EXTINCTION

EARTH • AT • RISK

Acid Rain

Alternative Sources of Energy

Animal Welfare

The Automobile and the Environment

Clean Air

Clean Water

Degradation of the Land

Economics of Environmental Protection

Environmental Action Groups

The Environment and the Law

Environmental Disasters

Extinction

The Fragile Earth

Global Warming

The Living Ocean

Nuclear Energy • Nuclear Waste

Overpopulation

The Ozone Layer

Recycling

The Rainforest

Solar Energy

Toxic Materials

What You Can Do for the Environment

EARTH • AT • RISK

EXTINCTION

by Rebecca Stefoff

Introduction by
Russell E. Train

Chairman of
the Board of Directors,
World Wildlife Fund and
The Conservation Foundation

CHELSEA HOUSE PUBLISHERS

new york philadelphia

5 7 9 8 6 4

Library of Congress Cataloging-in-Publication Data
Stefoff, Rebecca
Extinction/by Rebecca Stefoff; introduction by Russell E. Train.
p. cm.—(Earth at risk)
Includes index.
Summary: Examines the extinction of various plants and animals, humankind's effect on the biosphere and species loss, and the preservation and protection of life forms.
ISBN 0-7910-1578-5
0-7910-1603-X (paper)
1. Extinction (Biology)—Juvenile literature. [1. Extinction (Biology)] I. Title. II. Series. 91-2113
QE721.2.E97S75 1991 CIP
333.95137—dc20 AC

CONTENTS

INTRODUCTION

Russell E. Train

Administrator, Environmental Protection Agency, 1973 to 1977; Chairman of the Board of Directors, World Wildlife Fund and The Conservation Foundation

There is a growing realization that human activities increasingly are threatening the health of the natural systems that make life possible on this planet. Humankind has the power to alter nature fundamentally, perhaps irreversibly.

This stark reality was dramatized in January 1989 when *Time* magazine named Earth the "Planet of the Year." In the same year, the Exxon *Valdez* disaster sparked public concern over the effects of human activity on vulnerable ecosystems when a thick blanket of crude oil coated the shores and wildlife of Prince William Sound in Alaska. And, no doubt, the 20th anniversary celebration of Earth Day in April 1990 renewed broad public interest in environmental issues still further. It is no accident then that many people are calling the years between 1990 and 2000 the "Decade of the Environment."

And this is not merely a case of media hype, for the 1990s will truly be a time when the people of the planet Earth learn the meaning of the phrase "everything is connected to everything else" in the natural and man-made systems that sustain our lives. This will be a period when more people will understand that burning a tree in Amazonia adversely affects the global atmosphere just as much as the exhaust from the cars that fill our streets and expressways.

Central to our understanding of environmental issues is the need to recognize the complexity of the problems we face and the relationships between environmental and other needs in our society. Global warming provides an instructive example. Controlling emissions of carbon dioxide, the principal greenhouse gas, will involve efforts to reduce the use of fossil fuels to generate electricity. Such a reduction will include energy conservation and the promotion of alternative energy sources, such as nuclear and solar power.

The automobile contributes significantly to the problem. We have the choice of switching to more energy efficient autos and, in the longer run, of choosing alternative automotive power systems and relying more on mass transit. This will require different patterns of land use and development, patterns that are less transportation and energy intensive.

In agriculture, rice paddies and cattle are major sources of greenhouse gases. Recent experiments suggest that universally used nitrogen fertilizers may inhibit the ability of natural soil organisms to take up methane, thus contributing tremendously to the atmospheric loading of that gas—one of the major culprits in the global warming scenario.

As one explores the various parameters of today's pressing environmental challenges, it is possible to identify some areas where we have made some progress. We have taken important steps to control gross pollution over the past two decades. What I find particularly encouraging is the growing environmental consciousness and activism by today's youth. In many communities across the country, young people are working together to take their environmental awareness out of the classroom and apply it to everyday problems. Successful recycling and tree-planting projects have been launched as a result of these budding environmentalists who have committed themselves to a cleaner environment. Citizen action, activated by youthful enthusiasm, was largely responsible for the fast-food industry's switch from rainforest to domestic beef, for pledges from important companies in the tuna industry to use fishing techniques that would not harm dolphins, and the recent announcement by the McDonald's Corporation to phase out polystyrene "clam shell" hamburger containers.

Despite these successes, much remains to be done if we are to make ours a truly healthy environment. Even a short list of persistent issues includes problems such as acid rain, ground-level ozone and smog, and airborne toxins; ground water protection and nonpoint sources of pollution such as runoff from farms and city streets; wetlands protection; hazardous waste dumps; and solid waste disposal, waste minimization, and recycling.

Similarly, there is an unfinished agenda in the natural resources area: effective implementation of newly adopted management plans for national forests; strengthening the wildlife refuge system; national park management, including addressing the growing pressure of development on lands surrounding the parks; implementation of the Endangered Species Act; wildlife trade problems, such as that involving elephant ivory; and ensuring adequate sustained funding for these efforts at all levels of government. All of these issues are before us today; most will continue in one form or another through the year 2000.

Each of these challenges to environmental quality and our health requires a response that recognizes the complex nature of the problem. Narrowly conceived solutions will not achieve lasting results. Often it seems that when we grab hold of one part of the environmental balloon, an unsightly and threatening bulge appears somewhere else.

The higher environmental issues arise on the national agenda, the more important it is that we are armed with the best possible knowledge of the economic costs of undertaking particular environmental programs and the costs associated with not undertaking them. Our society is not blessed with unlimited resources, and tough choices are going to have to be made. These should be informed choices.

All too often, environmental objectives are seen as at cross purposes with other considerations vital to our society. Thus, environmental protection is often viewed as being in conflict with economic growth, with energy needs, with agricultural productions, and so on. The time has come when environmental considerations must be fully integrated into every nation's priorities.

One area that merits full legislative attention is energy efficiency. The United States is one of the least energy efficient of all the industrialized nations. Japan, for example, uses far less energy per unit of gross national product than the United States does. Of course, a country as large as the United States requires large amounts of energy for transportation. However, there is still a substantial amount of excess energy used, and this excess constitutes waste. More fuel efficient autos and home heating systems would save millions of barrels of oil, or their equivalent, each year. And air pollutants, including greenhouse gases, could be significantly reduced by increased efficiency in industry.

I suspect that the environmental problem that comes closest to home for most of us is the problem of what to do with trash. All over the world, communities are wrestling with the problem of waste disposal. Landfill sites are rapidly filling to capacity. No one wants a trash and garbage dump near home. As William Ruckelshaus, former EPA administrator and now in the waste management business, puts it, "Everyone wants you to pick up the garbage and no one wants you to put it down!"

At the present time, solid waste programs emphasize the regulation of disposal, setting standards for landfills and so forth. In the decade ahead, we must shift our emphasis from regulating waste disposal to an overall reduction in its volume. We must look at the entire waste stream, including product design and packaging. We must avoid creating waste in the first place. To the greatest extent possible, we should then recycle any waste that is produced. I believe that, while most of us enjoy our comfortable way of life and have no desire to change things, we also know in our hearts that our "disposable society" has allowed us to become pretty soft.

Land use is another domestic issue that might well attract legislative attention by the year 2000. All across the United States, communities are grappling with the problem of growth. All too often, growth imposes high costs on the environment—the pollution of aquifers; the destruction of wetlands; the crowding of shorelines; the loss of wildlife habitat; and the loss of those special places, such as a historic structure or area, that give a community a sense of identity. It is worth noting that growth is not only the product of economic development but of population movement. By the year 2010, for example, experts predict that 75% of all Americans will live within 50 miles of a coast.

It is important to keep in mind that we are all made vulnerable by environmental problems that cross international borders. Of course, the most critical global conservation problems are the destruction of tropical forests and the consequent loss of their biological capital. Some scientists have calculated extinction rates as high as 11 species per hour. All agree that the loss of species has never been greater than at the present time; not even the disappearance of the dinosaurs can compare to today's rate of extinction.

In addition to species extinctions, the loss of tropical forests may represent as much as 20% of the total carbon dioxide loadings to the atmosphere. Clearly, any international approach to the problem of global warming must include major efforts to stop the destruction of forests and to manage those that remain on a renewable basis. Debt-for-nature swaps, which the World Wildlife Fund has pioneered in Costa Rica, Ecuador, Madagascar, and the Philippines, provide a useful mechanism for promoting such conservation objectives.

Global environmental issues inevitably will become the principal focus in international relations. But the single overriding issue facing the world community today is how to achieve a sustainable balance between growing human populations and the earth's natural systems. If you travel as frequently as I do in the developing countries of Latin America, Africa, and Asia, it is hard to escape the reality that expanding human populations are seriously weakening the earth's resource base. Rampant deforestation, eroding soils, spreading deserts, loss of biological diversity, the destruction of fisheries, and polluted and degraded urban environments threaten to spread environmental impoverishment, particularly in the tropics where human population growth is greatest.

It is important to recognize that environmental degradation and human poverty are closely linked. Impoverished people desperate for land on which to grow crops or graze cattle are destroying forests and overgrazing even more marginal land. These people become trapped in a vicious downward spiral. They have little choice but to continue to overexploit the weakened resources available to them. Continued abuse of these lands only diminishes their productivity. Throughout the developing world, alarming amounts of land rendered useless by overgrazing and poor agricultural practices have become virtual wastelands, yet human numbers continue to multiply in these areas.

From Bangladesh to Haiti, we are confronted with an increasing number of ecological basket cases. In the Philippines, a traditional focus of U.S. interest, environmental devastation is widespread as deforestation, soil erosion, and the destruction of coral reefs and fisheries combine with the highest population growth rate in Southeast Asia.

Controlling human population growth is the key factor in the environmental equation. World population is expected to at least double to about 11 billion before leveling off. Most of this growth will occur in the poorest nations of the developing world. I would hope that the United States will once again become a strong advocate of international efforts to promote family planning. Bringing human populations into a sustainable balance with their natural resource base must be a vital objective of U.S. foreign policy.

Foreign economic assistance, the program of the Agency for International Development (AID), can become a potentially powerful tool for arresting environmental deterioration in developing countries. People who profess to care about global environmental problems—the loss of biological diversity, the destruction of tropical forests, the greenhouse effect, the impoverishment of the marine environment, and so on—should be strong supporters of foreign aid planning and the principles of sustainable development urged by the World Commission on Environment and Development, the "Brundtland Commission."

If sustainability is to be the underlying element of overseas assistance programs, so too must it be a guiding principle in people's practices at home. Too often we think of sustainable development only in terms of the resources of other countries. We have much that we can and should be doing to promote long-term sustainability in our own resource management. The conflict over our own rainforests, the old growth forests of the Pacific Northwest, illustrates this point.

The decade ahead will be a time of great activity on the environmental front, both globally and domestically. I sincerely believe we will be tested as we have been only in times of war and during the Great Depression. We must set goals for the year 2000 that will challenge both the American people and the world community.

Despite the complexities ahead, I remain an optimist. I am confident that if we collectively commit ourselves to a clean, healthy environment we can surpass the achievements of the 1980s and meet the serious challenges that face us in the coming decades. I hope that today's students will recognize their significant role in and responsibility for bringing about change and will rise to the occasion to improve the quality of our global environment.

Wounded by a massive harpoon, this injured and dying whale awaits final destruction by Japanese whalers.

chapter 1

THE LAST OF ITS KIND

A bird called the passenger pigeon once lived in the forests of North America. It numbered in the billions. It was without a doubt the most common bird in North America, and it may have been the most populous bird in the world. Twice each year, huge flocks of passenger pigeons, each flock numbering more than 100 million birds, flew across the land on their north-south migrations. The passage of a flock darkened the sky for hours, as though night had fallen in the middle of the day, and the sound of the wings was like "the roar of distant thunder," said 19th-century American naturalist John James Audubon, who witnessed several such migrations.

Unfortunately for the passenger pigeon, its meat was tasty. By the middle of the 19th century, the bird was considered a delicacy. Hunting took place on such a large scale that it amounted to wholesale slaughter. Hunters armed with shotguns and rifles waited in the forests where the passenger pigeons nested and, when the flocks alighted in the trees at dusk, opened fire. A typical hunting party of 3 or 4 men could bag 50,000 birds in a week; some shooters killed even more than that, partly for the money they made by selling the feathered carcasses to food dealers and partly for the sheer thrill of making a large kill. Although the flocks of passenger pigeons had seemed endless, the birds could not withstand the onslaught of human appetite combined with firearm technology, and their numbers dropped with startling rapidity. On March 24, 1900, a hunter shot the last known wild passenger pigeon. A few representatives of the species survived for a while in zoos. The last of these died on September 1, 1914, in the Cincinnati Zoo. On that date, the passenger pigeon became extinct.

The passenger pigeon is not the only creature whose extinction is well recorded in recent history. A similar fate overtook the great auk, a large seabird—much like the

The passenger pigeon, which once flew across North America in flocks numbering in the hundreds of millions, was hunted for its tasty meat and became extinct in 1914.

penguin—that once lived on the islands of the North Atlantic Ocean. Because these auks could not fly, they were easy prey for human hunters, who simply walked up to them and clubbed them to death. Sailors killed them for meat, and beginning in the 1750s feather hunters killed them for their soft, warm down, which was used to stuff pillows and mattresses. Throughout the early years of the 19th century, the great auks disappeared from one after another of their homes: Newfoundland, Scotland, and the Faeroe Islands, north of Great Britain. On June 3, 1844, on a small rocky island off the coast of Iceland, two fishermen killed the last breeding pair of great auks. The auks' nest contained one egg; the same fishermen smashed it. The great auk was extinct.

Birds are not the only creatures that have been driven to extinction by humankind. The Steller's sea cow was a large marine mammal—with a length of about 24 feet (7.3 meters)—that lived in a small region of the North Pacific Ocean, browsing on seaweed around the shores of several islands in the Bering Strait. It was named for Georg W. Steller, the scientist who discovered the species in 1741 during a voyage of exploration. Soon afterward, Russian seal hunters made a discovery of their own: They found that the Steller's sea cow was slow, unaggressive, and easily killed. By 1768, only 27 years after it had been discovered, the Steller's sea cow was wiped out forever.

It is perhaps easy to blame these extinctions on the unenlightened sailors and hunters of bygone eras. But that explanation does not account for the disappearance of the dusky seaside sparrow, a North American songbird. The last dusky seaside sparrow died in a wildlife park at Walt Disney World in Florida on June 16, 1987. The species had been effectively extinct even before that date, because the last six known survivors were

The great auk, a large, penguinlike seabird of the North Atlantic. The last great auks were killed in 1844.

all males. The dusky seaside sparrows were not clubbed or shot into extinction; they just ran out of places to live and breed as development turned more and more of the Atlantic seacoast over to human use.

On the other side of the world, the same fate awaits the Hawaiian honey eater, a species of bird called the *'o'o-'a'a* by the native Hawaiians, after its flutelike mating song. To the wildlife biologists at Alakai swamp on the Hawaiian island of Kauai, that song seems more melancholy each year. Since 1986, the last 'o'o-'a'a that is known to survive has sent out his mating call in vain, and scientists have given up hoping that a female 'o'o-'a'a will emerge from some remote hiding place to save the species from extinction. That male honey eater who sings alone in the swamp will be the last of his kind.

They probably cannot save the 'o'o-'a'a, but wildlife experts at the Olinda Endangered Species Captive Breeding Facility on the island of Maui are struggling to save the *'alala,* or Hawaiian crow, whose numbers have been reduced to about 15 by a disease that arrived in Hawaii in 1964 when a sick pheasant was imported to the islands from the Asian country of Nepal. The 'alala's prospects are grim. Disease has made some of the surviving birds sterile, and only three pairs are capable of breeding. Even if these Hawaiian crows produce healthy offspring, the birds will live out their lives in zoos or shelters. There is no longer any safe place to release them in the wild.

THREATENED, ENDANGERED, EXTINCT

Thousands of species of birds, plants, fish, reptiles, mammals, and insects around the world are in the same predicament as the Hawaiian crow, or are fast approaching it. Scientists cannot say for certain how many species are on the verge of vanishing—only that the number is probably greater than anyone suspects. Species that are known to be in real danger of becoming extinct are called *endangered* species; those whose numbers are dwindling and who may soon become endangered are called *threatened* species.

Some endangered species have become familiar as the subjects of television documentaries and newspaper headlines. The giant panda, a black-and-white bearlike mammal native to China, is one of the best-known endangered species. It has been adopted as the symbol of the World Wildlife Fund (WWF), an international conservation organization. During the 1970s, the WWF and other conservation organizations also drew the world's attention to the crisis of the tiger, which was threatened with extinction throughout Asia. Since then, stable populations of tigers have been established in a few protected parks, although some of the rarer varieties of these great cats, such as the Balinese and Caspian tigers, have disappeared or will probably soon do so. In the United States, there was a heated controversy during the 1980s over the fate of the California condor, a broad-winged vulture native to the American West that was nearly wiped out by a combination of hunting, land development that gobbled up its territory, and chemicals used by farmers that poisoned its food and killed its young. Debate raged first over whether the condor should be saved and then over how best to save it. The debate ended in 1987, when the last wild condor was captured as part of a captive breeding program. No California condors remain in the wild. Some conservationists are optimistic that the 30 or so condors that survive in zoos will breed healthy chicks that can one day be released into protected wild territory; others fear that the species will die out in captivity.

The animal that is most likely to serve as the focus of international concern about extinction during the 1990s is the African elephant, one of the most severely endangered creatures on the planet. Five hundred years ago, there were 10 million elephants in Africa. By 1979, there were about 1.3 million. By 1990, only 610,000 remained, and the number was falling fast. Ironically, the curved and pointed ivory tusks that served the elephant well as a defense against predators for many thousands of years have been its downfall in the modern world. Ornaments and art objects made of elephant ivory are highly prized by some

The last dusky seaside sparrow died in a wildlife park at Walt Disney World in Florida in 1987.

people, and although many nations have made it illegal to import or sell items made of ivory, poachers—that is, hunters who kill animals illegally—butcher 50,000 to 100,000 elephants every year to supply the international ivory trade. Kenya lost 75% of its elephants during the 1980s. Uganda lost 85% of its elephants between 1973 and 1990. It is quite possible that by the 21st century the huge and regal elephant, whose herds once seemed as essential and eternal a part of Africa as the majestic peaks of Mount Kilimanjaro, will survive only in a handful of heavily guarded wildlife parks and in the world's zoos.

The plight of the panda and the threat of extinction for the elephant catch the world's attention because pandas and elephants, like tigers and whales and mountain gorillas, are large mammals that most people readily recognize from books, television, or zoos. Many biologists and environmentalists, however, worry that the public's focus on "cuddly" or "likable" animals will draw attention away from other less glamorous endangered species, such as the plants, worms, beetles, and fungi that account for the majority of organisms in complete *ecosystems,* communities of organisms that are interdependent upon each other and their environment. In the spring and summer of 1990, for example, biologists from around the world began calling attention to the fact that almost all species of amphibians—animals such as frogs, toads, and salamanders that can live on land but spend part of their life cycle in the water—are getting rarer. Some species have recently become extinct, and others are on the verge of extinction. One example is the spotted leopard frog of North America, which until the 1970s was extremely common in every ditch and pond but is now hard to find in most parts of its range. Scientists warn that the population decline among amphibians could be a sign that environmental problems such as acid rain and water pollution are even more widespread than was believed. Furthermore, a fade-out of amphibians will affect other species as well. Insects will increase without amphibians to prey upon them, and at the same time there will be less food for the birds, small mammals, and reptiles that feed on amphibians.

The case of the vanishing frogs is a reminder that it is not only the highly visible creatures that are slipping toward extinction. Fish, reptiles, amphibians, insects, and plants are in at least as much trouble as birds and mammals. The crisis is at its worst in the world's tropical rainforests. These forests have the densest concentration of species of any environment on the planet. Hot, humid conditions and a stable climate are prime conditions for the proliferation of species. In a 2.5-acre (1-hectare) plot in Peru, for example, biologist Alwyn H. Gentry of the Missouri Botanical Garden identified more than 300 different kinds of trees; similarly, a single rainforest tree in Panama was found to contain more than 1,500 species of beetle. Although the rainforests of Central and South America, Africa, southern and southeastern Asia, and the Pacific region cover only about 6% of the earth's surface, they are home to at least 50% of all living species—perhaps, some scientists believe, as many as 80%. Most of these plants and animals have not yet been studied or even identified by biologists, yet the rainforests are being felled at a rapid rate for timber and to clear land for farming. Many species are thus being lost before they are found.

How fast are life-forms disappearing? E. O. Wilson, a biologist at Harvard University, believes that at least 4,000 to 6,000 species become extinct each year as a result of the destruction of the tropical rainforests alone; the actual worldwide extinction rate, he suggests, could be much higher. Peter Raven, the director of the Missouri Botanical Garden, estimates that species are becoming extinct at the rate of 100 per day, or 1 species about every 15 minutes. And Jared Diamond, a physiologist at the University of California in Los Angeles, predicts that if present trends continue at least 50% of all existing species will be either extinct or endangered by the year 2050.

SPECIES PRESENT AND PAST

In order to understand what extinction means, it is necessary to know something about how living things are organized into groups. The system of plant and animal classification that scientists use began to be developed around A.D. 1600 and is called *taxonomy.* The taxonomist's job is to identify the similarities among related organisms and the differences among unrelated ones. These similarities and differences are sometimes obvious, as in the distinction between plants that have flowers and plants that do not. Sometimes, however, the relationships among organisms are much less obvious, as in the recognition that horses are more closely related to rhinoceroses than they are to cows. The taxonomist places related organisms in large categories, which are in turn broken down into increasingly smaller categories. All living things belong to one of five kingdoms: plants, animals, fungi, or one of two kingdoms of tiny single-celled organisms, the Protista and Monera. The kingdoms are divided into phyla (the singular is phylum). The phyla are divided into classes, and so on through orders, families, genera (the singular is genus), and species. The species is the smallest taxonomic unit and the one that is most directly involved in present-day concerns about extinction.

The distinction between different species is not always clear-cut; roughly speaking, a species consists of all animals that, under natural conditions, can breed and produce offspring that are in turn capable of reproducing. Although lions and tigers can and sometimes do breed and produce offspring in zoos, they never do so in the wild, and so they cannot be considered members of the same species. Similarly, horses and donkeys breed and produce offspring called mules, but mules are sterile and cannot reproduce because horses and donkeys do not belong to the same species.

Many animals occur in several species; there are, for example, about 30 species of deer and 7 of tiger. Some species that are very similar to one another can breed and produce fertile offspring, but they rarely do so in the wild, and they may occupy separate geographic ranges. Some species are divided into two or more subspecies based on differences in appearance, such as variations in the color of feathers within a bird species. Subspecies of a given species can interbreed but generally do not do so in nature, usually because they live in different geographic regions. For all practical purposes, then, a species consists of the entire worldwide population of a particular plant or animal. Extinction occurs when all of the individual members of a species die.

Although species are the basic building blocks of taxonomy, scientists who study life and extinction often find it useful to talk in terms of larger categories, such as families. A family may include a handful of species or many thousands of species. For example, the giant panda of China is so different from all other animals that it has a species, a genus, and a family all to itself. If the giant panda becomes extinct, not just a single species but a whole family of life will have vanished from the earth.

No one knows for sure how many species exist today. After several centuries of systematic effort, scientists have identified and classified somewhere between 1.4 and 1.7 million distinct species of plants, insects, animals, fungi, algae, and

Terry L. Erwin of the Smithsonian Institution descends from the canopy of the Peruvian rainforest. Erwin's work with tropical insects led him to speculate that there might be at least 30 million species of living creatures in the world, more than 6 times the previously suspected total.

microorganisms. Biologists agree that this figure is not even close to the total number of species, but they do not yet agree on what that total might be. Cautious and conservative estimates place the total at about 4 or 5 million. Many biologists believe the true number to be much higher: 10 million or more. The highest estimate is that of Terry L. Erwin of the Smithsonian Institution's National Museum of Natural History, whose studies of insect populations in tropical rainforests have led him to suggest that the total number of living species on the planet is at least 30 million.

According to Robert M. May of Oxford University in England, the species that have been recorded are divided among the 5 kingdoms of living things as follows: The 2 kingdoms of single-celled organisms—Protista and Monera—together account for about 5% of all species, the fungal and plant kingdoms together account for another 22%, and animals account for the remaining 73%. Among the animals, however, there are only about 41,000 to 45,000 species of vertebrates (animals with spinal columns, namely fish, amphibians, reptiles, birds, and mammals). These include approximately 4,000 species of mammals, including bats and marine mammals such as whales and dolphins, and 9,000 species of birds. Both mammals and birds have been well studied. Although a few new bird and mammal species are identified each year, scientists do not expect to make numerous additions to these categories of animals. By far the greatest majority of known species are insects (there are approximately 750,000 of them), and most biologists feel that insects greatly predominate among the unknown species as well. Other species—both known and unknown—belong to such categories as spiders and mites, worms, corals, microscopic crustaceans on the ocean floor, fungi, and bacteria.

Although scientists do not know the number of species that now exist, they do know that the species alive today are only a tiny fraction of all the species that have ever lived. Paleontologists—scientists who study life-forms of the past—estimate that between 90% and 99% of all species that have ever existed are now extinct. This means that for every known living species, almost 100 species have become extinct. Some of these extinct species disappeared relatively recently; for example, the saber-toothed tiger of North and South America vanished only about 11,000 years ago and for a time shared the world with modern humans. But perhaps the best-known symbols of ancient extinction are the dinosaurs. Dinosaur species flourished all over the world for about 140 million years, until the last of them became extinct 65 million years ago, long before humans existed.

People have been studying the distant past and the earth's long history of life and death for several centuries. Their discoveries have shown that extinction is nothing new. The death of species has always been part of the history of life. In the great dinosaur extinction, for example, 75% of all animal species became extinct. But as an understanding of past extinctions will show, the crisis of endangered species in the 20th century is different from anything that has happened before to life on earth.

Charles Darwin (1809–82), the great English naturalist, was the first to publish a theory of biological evolution and to suggest how new species arise through the process of natural selection.

chapter 2

READING THE FOSSIL RECORD

Scientists have accumulated evidence that the earth is approximately 4.5 billion years old. They have also established that life arose fairly early in the history of the planet, probably about 3.5 billion years ago. For 3 billion years or so, the only forms of life were microscopic single-celled organisms, various types of ocean-dwelling bacteria and algae. Then, not much more than 600 million years ago, something new appeared in the earth's seas: animals with more than 1 cell. All the millions of species of plants and animals that have inhabited the earth—species both simple and complex, both alive and extinct—have lived and died in the past 600 million years or so.

Geology, which is the science of the earth and the processes that have formed it, and paleontology, the study of ancient life-forms based on fossils, are relatively new disciplines. The idea that the earth and life itself might be extremely old gradually developed during the 17th, 18th, and 19th centuries as people contemplated natural phenomena and shared their observations and conclusions with one another. New ideas about the origins of the earth and of life encountered a great deal of resistance, for they contradicted the centuries-old belief—based on certain ways of interpreting the Bible and other religious writings—that the earth was only a few thousand years old and that all living things had been created at the same time. Eventually, however, the new view of life framed by the pioneers of geology and paleontology gained general acceptance. A key element of that scientific vision is a concept that geologists call *deep time.*

THE DISCOVERY OF DEEP TIME

One of the first issues to engage the attention of investigators who were curious about the natural world was the puzzle of fossils. These are remnants or imprints of dead life-forms that are preserved in sedimentary rock or elsewhere in the earth's crust. Most fossils are of bones and shells, but some plants, soft fleshy animals, and even eggs, burrows, and footprints have been fossilized. In ancient times, people who found fossils thought that they were faulty or incomplete imitations of life that had occurred spontaneously in the earth. In medieval times, fossils were believed to be the remains of creatures that perished in the great flood recorded in the Old Testament of the Bible. During the Renaissance, Leonardo da Vinci (1452–1519) saw that fossil shells found high in the mountains were similar to well-known sea creatures such as clams, and he concluded that the peaks containing fossils of sea creatures must once have formed part of an ocean floor. Although the people of his era scoffed at the idea that mountains and seas could change places, geologists now know that Leonardo was correct. The contours of the earth have changed many times, and the continents have shifted their positions more than once.

Two 17th-century thinkers also examined the problem of fossils. The Englishman Robert Hooke (1635–1703) and the Dane Nicolas Steno (1638–86) proved that fossil shells were the remains of marine animals and that some of them were quite different from any creatures known to exist in modern times. Then, in the 18th century, the Scotsman James Hutton (1726–97) laid one of the foundations of modern geology. He was the first to suggest that the processes that shape the physical world, such as erosion and mountain building, must have been operating over almost unimaginably long periods of time. He wrote that "time . . . is to nature endless and as nothing," and he concluded his book *Theory of the Earth* (1795) with one of the most often quoted sentences in the history of science: "The result, therefore, of our present enquiry is, that we find no vestige of a beginning—no prospect of an end." These were disturbing words to many of the people of Hutton's time, who believed that time and the earth had begun not long before the start of human history, perhaps a few thousand or tens of thousands of years ago. But they were exciting words to fellow scientists, who were inspired to think of the earth's history in new, greatly expanded terms. Hutton's notion of vast periods of time stretching away in both directions from the present is what has come to be called deep time.

Deep time is sometimes called geologic time because the next developments in the study of the earth's history were concerned with establishing timetables for the ages and sequences of various types of rock. Geology and paleontology were closely related from the start. Using simple common sense, geologists reasoned that the deepest rocks were the oldest and that the topmost levels were the most recent. Before long, however, they discovered that the layers of buried rock had buckled, crumpled, and even folded over themselves in many places, so that the different layers, or strata, were often jumbled. They also found that one of the most useful tools for identifying rock strata was the fossil content of the rocks. Certain strata of buried rock contained the same kinds of fossils in widely separated parts of the world. Some scientists began studying and classifying fossils, and people in general began to be interested in these records of vanished life; dinosaur fossils, in particular, aroused astonishment and wonder, just as they continue to do today.

In 1799, an English surveyor named William Smith published the first stratigraphic chart, which showed the various layers of rock, clay, and soil that lay under the surface of the British Isles. But it was with the publication of the British scientist Charles Lyell's three-volume *Principles of Geology* in 1830–33 that geology really took its place among the established sciences. One of Lyell's accomplishments was to begin devising a systematic framework for discussions of past time. Using the fossils of ancient shells as a guide, he identified three epochs of the distant past, which he called the Eocene (dawn of recent, in Latin), Miocene (middle of recent), and Pliocene (almost recent) epochs. These names are still used, although the geologic time scale has grown more detailed since Lyell's day. Scientists now divide all past time into three major eras. These are preceded by what is called the Precambrian time, which began with the formation of the planet and continued until 570 million years ago, just after complex life-forms had appeared. The Precambrian time is followed by the Paleozoic era (*paleozoic* means old life), which

Sir Charles Lyell (1797–1875), the Scottish geologist whose Principles of Geology *put forward the view of the uniformitarians, believed that both geologic and biological changes took place slowly and evenly over long periods of time.*

lasted until 225 million years ago. The next era is the Mesozoic (middle life), which ended about 65 million years ago. The Cenozoic era (recent life) began then and is still going on. Geologists have divided each era into periods, and they have further subdivided some of the periods into smaller units called epochs.

The divisions between eras, periods, and epochs are based on the fossil records of life-forms that arose in each new phase—or, in some cases, on the extinctions that are recorded in the fossil record. For example, one of the marks of the boundary between the Permian and the Triassic periods about 225 million years ago is the disappearance of all species of trilobites, sea-dwelling creatures similar to present-day horseshoe crabs. These animals flourished in the earth's seas from the beginning of

GEOLOGICAL TIME SCALE

Era	Period	Epoch	Millions of Years Ago
Cenozoic	Quaternary	Holocene or Recent Pleistocene	
			1.5 to 2
	Tertiary	Pliocene Miocene Oligocene Eocene Paleocene	
			65
Mesozoic	Cretaceous Jurassic Triassic		
			225
Paleozoic	Permian Pennsylvanian* Mississippian Devonian Silurian Ordovician Cambrian		
			570
Precambrian (back to 3.5 billion years ago...?)			

*The Pennsylvanian and Mississippian periods are sometime considered one category, the Carboniferous period.

Adapted from Wonderful Life: The Burgess Shale and the Nature of History *by Stephen Jay Gould. Reprinted by permission of W. W. Norton Co., Inc.*

the Cambrian period to the end of the Permian, when they became extinct. The disappearance of the trilobites is just one of many extinctions that serve as landmarks in time.

EVOLUTION AND EXTINCTION

The work of Hutton, Lyell, and others established the concept of deep time, but scientists are still trying to discover just how geologic and biological processes operate over long time spans. One early debate concerned the rate and nature of change in geologic time. Lyell held that geologic and paleontological changes occur very slowly and steadily as the result of gradual, evenly paced processes, such as the eroding of soil by rainfall and the depositing of sediment on the ocean bottom. The scientists who shared Lyell's opinion that change occurs at a slow, uniform rate were called *uniformitarians.*

The uniformitarians were challenged by the *catastrophists,* scientists who believed that changes happen

Baron Georges Cuvier (1769–1832), founder of the science of comparative anatomy and an early catastrophist, believed that geologic and biological changes occurred rapidly and violently. Actually, Cuvier was a religious fundamentalist who believed that, as in Genesis, periodic floods killed off species, after which God would create new ones.

suddenly and abruptly in response to isolated catastrophes, such as floods, volcanic eruptions, and ice ages. The leading catastrophists of Lyell's time were Baron Georges Cuvier (1769–1832) and Louis Agassiz (1807–73), both of whom were fossil experts. Although the debate between the uniformitarians and the catastrophists was a heated one for many years, modern geologists feel that both groups were right. Geologic change *does* take place slowly and steadily over long periods of time, but sudden cataclysms do occur, and they also contribute to the shape and structure of the earth.

The debate between uniformitarians and catastrophists was concerned with plants and animals as much as with rocks. Paleontologists and biologists wondered—and are still wondering—exactly how and why species appear and then become extinct. Do changes in the *biosphere*, that part of the earth and atmosphere inhabited by living things, occur slowly and steadily, or abruptly? For a time, it was generally believed that species were fixed and unchanging, although no one could satisfactorily explain how or why they came into being or why so many species had vanished from the earth, as the study of fossils showed. Then, in the middle of the 19th century, the English naturalists Charles Darwin (1809–82) and Alfred Russel Wallace (1823–1913) developed a set of new ideas about the relationships among species. These ideas are called the theory of evolution. Darwin is considered the principal founder of evolutionary thought because his book *On the Origin of Species* (1859) was the first and most important expression of the theory.

The central notion of evolution is that species change over long periods of time as a result of slight changes that distinguish an individual organism from others of its species.

These changes are called mutations and are now known to be caused by random minor variations in organisms' DNA (deoxyribonucleic acid), the complex genetic material that contains an identity code for each living thing. Darwin realized that variations—such as thicker fur or teeth of a slighty different shape—can be transmitted to an organism's offspring. He also saw that most organisms produce more offspring than can possibly survive to adulthood, so that existence could be viewed as a constant struggle for survival. He formulated the principal of *natural selection*, an important part of the theory of evolution stating that variations that help an organism are more likely to be passed on to later generations than are variations that hurt the organism or have no noticeable effect on it. The giraffe is a good illustration of this concept. Biologists believe that a genetic mutation that made some giraffes' necks longer enabled them to forage for food in higher branches where others could not reach. Those animals with this advantage could feed better and live longer than giraffes without it, so they could produce more offspring. The neck mutation was reproduced in these offspring, which in turn had an advantage over other giraffes and produced more offspring. After many generations, the long-necked giraffes outnumbered those with shorter necks and eventually replaced them altogether.

Darwin's revolutionary insight was that species can change, or evolve, into new species. He was the first to suggest that *all* species, whether current or extinct, are related to one another by descent from the same extremely remote ancestral life-forms, which over long periods of time had evolved into all the different species. These ideas were hard for many people to accept, and opposition to Darwin's thinking continued into the

20th century. Today, however, all reputable geologists, paleontologists, and biologists agree on the general idea of evolution, although they are still working out the details of how it works.

Among the most recent theories about evolution is one developed by Niles Eldredge of the American Museum of Natural History and Stephen Jay Gould of Harvard University. Their studies of the fossil record suggest that *speciation*, or the formation of new species, does not take place at a uniform rate.

Louis Agassiz (1807–73) studied under Cuvier and spent the last 25 years of his life teaching at Harvard University. His study of glaciers and fossils led him to support the theory of catastrophism.

Eldredge and Gould propose that for most of the time, the majority of species undergo little change and new species arise infrequently, slowly, and gradually, at an even rate. Occasionally, however, there are bursts of speciation, periods in which many new species and whole families of genera and species arise with relative suddenness. The two scientists use the term *punctuated equilibrium* to describe their theory that the number of species generally remains about the same, in a state of equilibrium, for long stretches of time, which are punctuated, or broken up, by bursts of more rapid speciation. Because these periods of rapid speciation often occur just *after* a number of earlier species have become extinct, Eldredge and Gould are among the many scientists of various disciplines who are now turning their attention to the topic of extinction. Indeed, one of the biggest unanswered questions of paleontology concerns extinction: What really caused the deaths of all the species and families of species that have disappeared from the earth during the long history of life?

The principles of evolution and natural selection suggest that a species becomes extinct when it can no longer compete with other species that are better suited to survival. But surprising geologic and paleontological discoveries in the 1980s have hatched a brood of new theories about ancient extinctions. These theories suggest that species do not necessarily disappear because they are less fit for survival—just less fortunate. Scientists are eagerly searching the fossil record for evidence to support these new ideas. They hope to fill in some of the blank spots on the map of history—and perhaps to solve one of the most puzzling mysteries of science: What killed the dinosaurs?

A reconstruction, from the Tyrrell Museum of Paleontology in Alberta, Canada, of the skeleton of Tyrannosaurus rex, *a carnivorous dinosaur that became extinct about 65 million years ago.*

chapter 3

THE GREAT DYINGS

Ever since paleontologists began fitting together fossil bones to reconstruct dinosaurs, people have been fascinated by these giant creatures. The term *dinosaur* covers a multitude of species belonging to many families. The first of them arose about 220 million years ago. Some dinosaurs were armed with horns or covered with armor plates; some, like the *Tyrannosaurus rex,* were ferocious and predatory, with massive teeth and claws; some were gigantic, peaceful herbivores (plant eaters); and some were small, rapid runners, not much larger than chickens or dogs. Their cousins soared through the prehistoric skies and swarmed in the seas. For decades, museumgoers have marveled at the skeletons of these archaic beasts and wondered why they became extinct.

The dinosaurs got their start during the Triassic period. Although some dinosaur species vanished as others emerged, the dinosaur group as a whole flourished for more than 150 million years. But 65 million years ago, the last remaining dinosaurs—perhaps 100 or so species—became extinct. Many theories have been advanced to account for the dinosaurs' extinction. Some of these ideas are absurd, such as the suggestion that the dinosaurs died out because they got so large and clumsy that they could no longer mate and reproduce. Other theories have seemed more plausible, only to be discarded because they could not be tested or because scientific evidence contradicted them. Among these theories is the notion that mammals, which were small and ratlike during the age of dinosaurs, killed off the giant reptiles by eating their eggs; another idea is that the dinosaurs died of poisoning or drug overdoses after eating the new species of flowering plants that were springing up in all parts of the world. Many theories about dinosaur extinction have suggested some sort of global climate change. The dinosaurs might have been killed off, for example, if advancing glaciers swept the earth into an ice age or if rising temperatures dried up the swamps and grasslands where they lived. One of the most enduring popular images of the dinosaurs' end is found in Walt Disney's classic animated film *Fantasia* (1940): One tragic and moving scene shows anguished dinosaurs lurching to their death across a parched desert landscape, under a burning sun.

No one knows which of these theories, if any, is true. But in the 1970s and 1980s, scientists put forward several new ideas about the disappearance of the dinosaurs and other vanished forms of life. These new ideas are shedding light on some of the most baffling and mysterious events in the history of life, episodes of widespread death and destruction that are called mass extinctions.

For a long time, paleontologists have known that the fossil record shows a handful of episodes of sudden, widespread extinction—relatively short spans of time during which a large percentage of the earth's species became extinct. Scientists have used some of these mass extinctions to mark the beginnings and ends of geologic periods. For example, the Ordovician extinction, about 440 million years ago, marks the boundary between the Ordovician and Silurian periods. Life was confined to the seas at the time. The earliest ancestors of fish and corals survived the extinction, but many species of marine invertebrates (species without a spinal column) and reef-building organisms similar to corals did not. A second mass extinction, called the late Frasnian extinction, took place about 370 million years ago, near the end of the Devonian period. It killed many species of fish and about 70% of the invertebrate sea creatures that made up the bulk of living creatures on the planet.

The most devastating of all extinctions occurred about 225 million years ago, at the end of the Permian period and the beginning of the Triassic period. Somewhere between 80% and 96% of all living species perished. Because life had got a toehold on the land by this time, the Permian extinction affected land dwellers as well as sea dwellers. Insects, amphibians, plants, and several families of creatures that scientists call mammal-like reptiles perished in the great dying. During the Permian period, there were between 45,000 and 240,000 species on earth. David Raup of the University of Chicago has estimated that the Permian extinction left only 1,800 to 9,600 of these species alive to serve as the basis for all later life. Some of the mammal-like reptiles survived to dominate the Triassic period. But even though these reptiles were numerous and well established during the Triassic, some new groups—dinosaurs, mammals, and crocodiles—began to emerge in that period.

The mammal-like reptiles were completely wiped out in the next major mass extinction, which occurred at the end of the Triassic period, about 200 million years ago. This Triassic extinction killed about 75% of sea-dwelling species and some land-dwelling species. The dinosaurs, crocodiles, and mammals, however, survived. During the Jurassic period, which followed the Triassic extinction, the mammals retained a small population while the dinosaurs diversified into many families and covered the earth. Some families of dinosaurs, such as the brontosauruses, were huge. But the brontosaurus, as well as the armored stegosaurus and the large, carnivorous allosaurus, became extinct at the end of the Jurassic period, about 140 million years ago. The dinosaurs that ruled the Cretaceous period, which followed the Jurassic, were the tyrannosaurus, the horned triceratops, and various species of hadrosaurs, or duck-billed dinosaurs.

The final death of the dinosaurs took place at the end of the Cretaceous period. The K-T boundary is the name scientists have given to this mass extinction, which marks the boundary between the Cretaceous period and the following Tertiary period. The K-T extinction killed about a third of all species, mostly sea dwellers. Plankton, corals, giant reef-building clams, all large marine reptiles, and a host of other marine species died out. On land, the dinosaurs and their flying cousins, the winged pterodactyls, vanished. Turtles, crocodiles, small lizards, and flowering plants survived. So did most species of mammals. The mammals had been small and obscure since their origin millions

An artist's conception of a stegosaurus, a large, partially armored dinosaur that became extinct about 140 million years ago.

of years earlier in the Triassic period, but after the disappearance of the dinosaurs they blossomed, diversifying into numerous new families and species, from bats to whales. Fish species also increased and diversified after the K-T extinction. Just as the Triassic mass extinction appears to have paved the way for the age of the dinosaurs by killing off the mammal-like reptiles, the K-T extinction apparently set the stage for the age of mammals by killing off the dinosaurs.

NEW THEORIES

Since the 1970s, advances in geologic knowledge have led to new ideas about the mass extinctions. Geologists now know that the earth's surface consists of a dozen or so very large, flat plates of rock that rest on the hot molten rock of the planet's interior. The theory of *plate tectonics* explains how these plates drift very, very slowly around the world, propelled by forces that move the molten matter underneath them. As the plates move, they carry the earth's continents with them. The continents that are now spaced around the planet have been in different positions at various times in the past, and several times in the world's history they have been joined together into huge landmasses that geologists call supercontinents.

Many scientists today think that the effects of plate tectonics are responsible for at least some of the mass extinctions. At the time of the Ordovician extinction, for example, the present-day continents of Africa, South America, Australia, and Antarctica were joined in a single supercontinent that has been named Gondwana. The extinction was probably triggered by climate changes that occurred over a 5-million-year period as Gondwana drifted over the South Pole and became very cold. The increasing cold made glaciers form; this drew water from the global seas and cooled the whole planet, bringing death to many life-forms that were adapted to life in warm, shallow waters. Gondwana drifted over the South Pole again about 70 million years later, perhaps setting off another period of glaciation that could account for the late Frasnian extinction.

The biggest of all the mass extinctions, the Permian (225 million years ago), may have been caused by the biggest event in the history of plate tectonics. All of the present-day continents were joined into a single enormous supercontinent that scientists call Pangaea. This caused profound disturbances in the temperature and depth of the seas as well as in land temperatures. Paleontologist Bob Sloan of the University of Minnesota claims that the great Permian mass extinction actually occurred in phases, or pulses—at least 6 distinct phases of extinction spread over the final 8 million years of the Permian period, corresponding to wild climate changes that were caused by the slow movement of Pangaea in and out of the 2 polar regions.

In 1980, scientists led by the father-and-son team of Walter and Luis Alvarez of the University of California at Berkeley published a new theory about the K-T extinction that killed the dinosaurs. In the course of geologic excavations in Italy and elsewhere, the Alvarezes found a surprisingly large amount of iridium in a layer of the earth that corresponds roughly to the boundary between the Cretaceous and the Tertiary periods 65 million years ago. Iridium is a metallic element related to platinum; it is very rare on the earth's surface but occurs in higher concentrations in objects from space, such as meteorites. The Alvarezes and their colleagues concluded that the iridium at the K-T line must have been brought to earth by a large object from space. They determined that around 66 million years ago the earth was struck by an asteroid about 6 miles (10 kilometers) in diameter. The force of the impact caused the asteroid to explode, sending an enormous cloud of iridium-enriched dust into the air; if the impact occurred at sea, the heat of the asteroid sent water vapor high into the atmosphere. Either way, the skies were dark for a long time—one to three months. Temperatures fell suddenly and dramatically. Fire storms, like those that raged in Yellowstone National Park in the summer of 1988, may have spread across the whole planet, destroying as much as 90% of its forests. Plants in the sea and on land that depend on sunlight would have died, and the animals that ate those plants and each other would have died, too. The K-T extinction struck earth suddenly and from outside, like the blow of a cosmic hammer.

This *impact* theory, as it is called, stirred up a storm of research and debate among geologists, astronomers, paleontologists, and biologists. Many scientists were impressed by the evidence that supports the impact theory and now agree that the K-T extinction—and perhaps other mass extinctions—were caused by extraterrestrial objects, possibly comets, striking the earth. Iridium has been found in Australia at a level that corresponds with the late Frasnian mass extinction in the Devonian period. Helmut Geldsetzer of the Geologic Survey of Canada has studied Devonian fossils in the Canadian Rockies, and he suggests that the marine invertebrates and reef builders that lived in the warm, shallow waters near the seacoasts of this period might have died after an asteroid plunged into the deep central ocean, sending surges of icy water from the depths up into the shallows. Charles Sandberg of the U.S. Geological Survey has found evidence that violent storms and tidal waves tore across the earth at around the time of the late Frasnian extinction, and he feels that they may have been caused by a group of comets or asteroids passing nearby and disturbing the earth's tides with the pull of their gravity.

The impact theory has also been linked to the Triassic extinction 200 million years ago. In the rugged, desolate center of Quebec province in Canada is a lake called Manicouagan. The lake is actually part of a large crater that was made when some huge object crashed into the earth. One study dates the Manicouagan crater at 210 million years old, but paleontologist Paul Olsen of Columbia University believes that the impact occurred closer to the Triassic extinction and caused that mass dying. As far as the K-T extinction is concerned, there are several candidates for the site of the impact. Some geologists feel that a large extraterrestrial object struck what is now India, causing volcanic eruptions and lava flows and setting off the K-T dying.

Others point to the town of Manson, Iowa, which sits in the center of a massive crater that has been shown to be 66 million years old. If the Manson crater was caused by the impact of an object from space, its timing would have been about right for the K-T extinction. And in December of 1990, scientists announced the discovery of a huge impact crater on Mexico's Yucatán Peninsula. Preliminary tests showed the crater to be between 65 and 66 million years old.

Not all scientists have jumped onto the impact bandwagon. Many paleontologists and others feel that extraterrestrial agents are not needed to account for the mass extinctions. They say that forces at work right here on earth, such as plate tectonics and climate change, could do the job. In some ways, the debate resembles the one between the uniformitarians and the catastrophists concerning rates of geologic change. The impact enthusiasts suggest that the mass dyings might have been triggered by events that would seem sudden even in the context of a human life. "At most we are dealing with 20,000 years—and maybe just one stormy night," states Willi Ziegler of the Senckenberg Museum in Frankfurt, Germany, talking about the Triassic extinction. But more traditional scientists point to evidence that the great extinctions, although they *were* quite

An artist's conception of a pterodactyl, a prehistoric flying lizard that vanished at the end of the Cretaceous period about 65 million years ago.

rapid in terms of the geologic time scale, nevertheless happened over periods of a million years or more. By the end of the 1980s, the majority of scientists had taken up a position somewhere in the middle. It is now generally accepted that some impacts have occurred, dramatically affecting the life and death of species, but that climate changes and other slow-acting factors have also been important in staging the mass extinctions.

The study of mass extinctions took a big step forward in 1982, when David Raup and John Sepkoski of the University of Chicago published the results of a detailed study of the fossil record. Using computers, they assembled 150 years' worth of information about fossils. They then scanned the fossil record for patterns, trying to determine how many families of organisms became extinct in each million-year period. They came up with a few surprises. For one thing, they established what they call the background rate of extinction—that is, a normal rate of extinction that remains fairly steady throughout all of geologic time. The mass extinctions stand out sharply in contrast to this background rate. The background rate of extinction ranges from 2.0 to 4.6 families of organisms lost each million years, but during the mass extinctions the rate shoots to as high as 19.3 families per million years.

Raup and Sepkoski discovered that the fossil record is dotted with many more mass extinctions than the handful that scientists have always recognized. Their study suggests that mass extinctions have occurred about every 26 million years throughout geologic time. Not all of these extinctions have been as big or as bad as the Permian, the K-T, and other well-known die-offs, but they can clearly be seen against the background rate. The most startling and mysterious feature of this view of extinction is the regularity of its cycle. Some scientists have suggested that the earth periodically passes through clusters of comets, and astronomers are searching the heavens for something that could cause comet showers every 26 million years. It has been suggested that the showers might be caused by the movements of an unknown 10th planet at the outer limits of the solar system or of a dark star that is a companion to the sun, but no answers have yet been found. It appears that the study of mass extinction will continue to be one of the most active areas in all of science for some time to come. As geologist Bevan French of the National Aeronautics and Space Administration says, "These are exciting times to be looking at extinction."

If Raup and Sepkoski's theory about 26-million-year cycles of mass extinction is correct, then an extinction about 14 million years ago was the most recent one. This means that the earth does not have to face the next mass extinction in the cycle for 12 million years. This should be good news. But a new kind of mass extinction is under way, and it has nothing to do with comets or asteroids, plate tectonics or glaciers. The current mass extinction is different from anything that has happened to life before. The *rate* of species loss is unprecedentedly high—perhaps 400 times the normal background rate. And for the first time a single species is responsible for wiping out species after species of the plants and animals with which it shares the world. That destructive species is *Homo sapiens*, or humankind, and its activities are bringing about a new era of mass dying. This time, no one has to search the distant reaches of the solar system or the caverns of the seafloor for clues about the causes of the extinctions—the responsibility lies much closer to home.

An orangutan in Tangung Puting National Park in Indonesia; this species is increasingly threatened by habitat destruction.

chapter 4

HUMANKIND AND MASS EXTERMINATION

Naturalist Alfred Russel Wallace, one of the first proponents of the theory of evolution, once wrote that human beings live in "a zoologically impoverished world, from which all the hugest, and fiercest, and strangest forms have recently disappeared." Wallace was referring not to the long-ago extinction of the dinosaurs but to a wave of extinctions that took place in the very recent past, near the end of the Pleistocene epoch—between 13,000 and 11,000 years ago, as the glaciers of the last ice age retreated poleward. Unlike the great mass extinctions of the distant past, the Pleistocene extinction did not affect marine creatures or plants, and it affected few birds or small animals. The Pleistocene extinction seemed to concentrate on what zoologists call the megafauna—that is, big animals that weigh 100 pounds (37.3 kilograms) or more.

The plains and forests of the Pleistocene world swarmed with large mammals that are known today only from fossils and from fragments of skins and bodies preserved in caves and tar pits. Carnivores such as the saber-toothed tigers and dire wolves;

giant ground-dwelling sloths related to the present-day tree sloths of South America; beavers the size of bears; long-haired mammoths and mastodons like sturdy, shaggy elephants; and glyptodonts, armadillo-like creatures with tough skins like shells—all of these roamed North and South America. Australia had its own Pleistocene megafauna, which included procoptodons, the largest members of the kangaroo family that ever lived, and diprotodons, grazing marsupials as large as today's rhinoceroses. By about 11,000 years ago, all of these creatures had vanished.

For a long time, Alfred Russel Wallace thought that the Pleistocene extinction of megafauna was connected with the end of the Ice Age, which must have introduced widespread changes in climate and vegetation patterns, bringing warmer and wetter summers and colder winters. But by the time of his death in 1913, he had revised his thinking. Bones of humans found together with those of mammoths showed that people lived side by side with the Pleistocene megafauna and that early hunters were capable of bringing down such prey as mammoths with spears. Wallace and others began to think that the extinction of large animals at the end of the Pleistocene epoch was caused by human hunters.

This idea is called the *overkill* theory. Its leading modern advocate is Paul Martin, an ecologist at the University of Arizona. Martin claims that Africa, Asia, and Europe lost relatively few species during Pleistocene times because these were the continents of human evolution, and over thousands of generations the animals had learned to be wary of people, who were just another part of a long-established ecosystem. But Australia and the Americas, as well as the islands of the Pacific Ocean, were lands of human colonization. People with sophisticated cultures

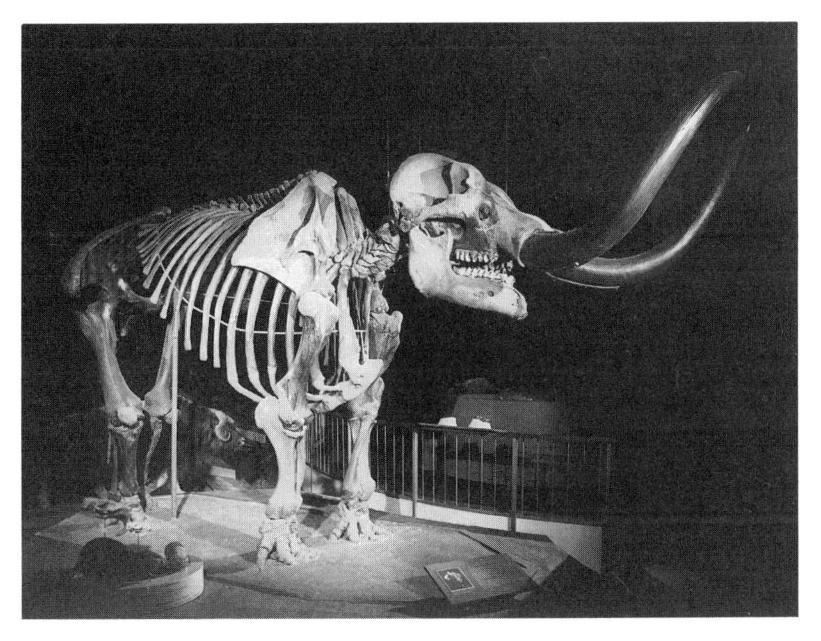

A reconstruction of the skeleton of a mastodon, which many scientists believe was hunted to extinction by early human beings.

and hunting skills appeared in these lands fairly suddenly and in well-organized groups late in the Pleistocene epoch. They killed large animals for food, reducing the numbers of some species so severely that those species could not breed enough young to keep going. Physiologist Jared Diamond supports the overkill theory. According to Diamond, 73% of large North American mammals became extinct right around the time humans arrived on their continent. The figure was even higher in South America (80%) and Australia (86%).

A number of scientists feel that Martin is wrong about the human overkilling of Pleistocene mammals. They claim that climate changes caused by the receding glaciers, or perhaps damage to the atmosphere caused by an exploding star somewhere in the vicinity of the solar system, brought about the extinction of the megafauna. The issue is not likely to be settled without prolonged investigation. But Martin points out that even in recent historical times, the intrusion of humans into new ecosystems has led to extinctions. For example, the giant lemur was a tree-dwelling primate, distantly related to the remote ancestors of apes, monkeys, and humans, that lived on the Indian Ocean island of Madagascar. It became extinct very soon after the first humans arrived in Madagascar about 1,500 years ago, and other species of lemur have been driven into extinction, or to the edge of it, since then. Moas were giant flightless birds more than 10 feet (approximately 3 meters) tall that lived on the islands of New Zealand in the South Pacific Ocean. The Maori people, New Zealand's first human colonists, reached the islands 1,000 years ago, and before long the moas had disappeared; old Maori ovens are filled with roasted moa bones. The urus, a relative of the domestic ox, lived in the forests of prehistoric Europe and stood 6 feet (1.83 meters) tall at the shoulder. It was hunted to extinction during the Middle Ages as the human population of the continent swelled and the forests were cut down. The list goes on and on, up to the ill-fated Steller's sea cow that was killed off in the North Pacific Ocean in the 18th century and the great auk that disappeared from the North Atlantic in the 19th. Today, the list includes thousands of endangered species, such as the white-winged guan, a turkeylike bird that has been overhunted in its native Peru. In 1989, there were about 100 guans left alive.

Whether or not they share Martin's belief that human hunters caused the Pleistocene extinctions, virtually all scientists agree that humankind has had—and is continuing to have—a devastating effect upon other forms of life on earth. The problem has to do with the growth of the human population, which has multiplied and spread over the planet in a hardy, resilient way that humans themselves usually associate with weeds or pests. Fifty thousand years ago, there were perhaps several million people on the planet. By the year 1600, there were 500 million, or half a billion. By 1990 there were more than 5 billion. The United Nations Population Fund research group predicts that the global population will double to 10 billion people by the year 2027. The increase in the number of people puts the squeeze on plants and animals in a number of indirect and direct ways.

PATHS TO EXTINCTION

Species can become extinct for many reasons, some of which are independent of human activity. The natural processes that can lead to extinction are not yet well understood by researchers. But the overwhelming majority of extinctions in modern times are caused by people. They fall into four general categories: introduction, habitat destruction, the domino effect, and overhunting.

Introduction. Human beings are nearly always accompanied in their travels by other kinds of animals—cats, dogs, rats, domestic livestock, and insects such as fleas and lice. In the course of their travels around the world, people have introduced their companion species into many ecosystems where they did not previously exist. The result has always been disaster for other species. In New Zealand, for example, there were no cats or dogs until white settlers came there from Europe. Once they were introduced, however, the cats and dogs flourished because the local ecosystem did not contain any animals that

continued on page 58

DEAD BRANCHES ON HUMANITY'S FAMILY TREE

Human beings have brought extinction to many other species. Yet humans are animals, part of the natural world with a long evolutionary history, although their consciousness and their ability to develop cultures make them different from all other forms of life. As part of the animal world, humans have been subjected to the same forces that have shaped other species—including extinction.

People belong to a group of mammals called primates, which also includes lemurs, apes, and monkeys as well as all their ancestors. Primates are a very old group. However, hominids, as the upright-walking primates are called, developed only a few million years ago. The particular group of hominids from which humans are descended probably split off from the families that ultimately produced chimpanzees and orangutans sometime around 5 to 8 million years ago. The earliest known hominid fossils that are recognizable as human ancestors were found in Ethiopia and Kenya, in east Africa. They are

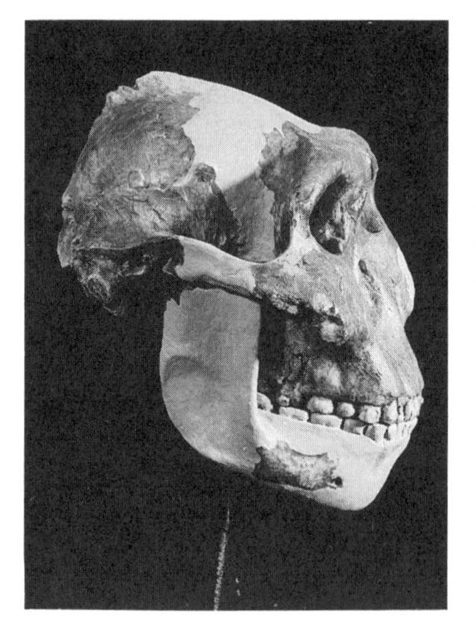

The skull of Australopithecus robustus, *one of the earliest human ancestors. This individual lived in East Africa more than 4 million years ago.*

about 4 million years old and belong to creatures called australopithecines. The story of how the australopithecine fossils were discovered in the 1970s and 1980s is one of the most exciting scientific adventures of all time, involving rivalry, trickery, detective work, and a good deal of luck. Two books that tell the story of this adventure are *Lucy: The Beginnings of Humankind* by Donald Johanson and Maitland Edey and *The People of the Lake: Mankind and Its Beginnings* by Richard Leakey and Roger Lewin.

With humans, as with other species, evolution and extinction seem to involve some degree of luck. Research by paleontologist Elisabeth S. Vrba of Yale University and other scientists suggests that global coolings millions of years ago caused African forests to be supplanted by grasslands, favoring the survival of apes that could walk on two legs and use their hands to forage more effectively. Who knows what sort of hominid species—if any—might have flourished had climatic changes been different?

More than one species of australopithecines roamed the African plains. Present-day humans are descended from one branch of the australopithecine family, but another branch, whose members had large jaws and teeth and apparently ate only vegetation, somehow became extinct about 1 million years ago. The two branches of the australopithecine family appear to have lived side by side for several million years. Paleontologists have not yet been able to determine why one branch survived and eventually developed into *Homo sapiens*, or present-day humans, and the other branch dwindled and died out.

Something similar happened in Europe much more recently. *Homo sapiens* existed in two versions that were quite different in appearance, although both belonged to the same species. One subspecies—with short legs, a large brain case, and a backward-sloping brow—is called Neanderthal man. The other—taller, with a more rounded brow, and in every way identical to present-day people—is called Cro-Magnon man. These 2 types of humans seem to have overlapped in time and space until about 35,000 years ago, when the Neanderthals became extinct. Were they felled by disease? Did the Cro-Magnons kill them or perhaps absorb them through interbreeding? Many theories have been advanced, but—although the age of Neanderthal man is only the blink of an eye away in geologic time—no one knows.

continued from page 55
could compete with them. Species that had lived in New Zealand for centuries, such as a large ground-dwelling parrot called the kakapo, were gobbled up by these new predators. Ocean islands all over the world have suffered from introduced species. Sailors used to stock islands with goats and pigs to provide future provisions, and these animals, along with rats, managed to destroy species of plants, birds, and animals that had never had to cope with predators like them before.

Sometimes the species that are introduced by man carry disease. A diseased pheasant from Nepal may have caused the virtual extermination of the Hawaiian crow. A fungal blight that was accidentally introduced to North America has almost wiped out the American chestnut tree. And sometimes the introductions are deliberate, intended to result in some benefit to mankind. A large edible fish called the Nile perch was introduced to Lake Victoria, in eastern Africa, in the hope that it might provide a good food source and a new fishing industry for the people of the region. In this case, the road to extinction was paved with good intentions. Although the Nile perch has flourished in the lake, it is devouring the hundreds of fish species that are native to the lake, most of which occur nowhere else on earth and many of which had great value as food or aquarium fish. In the April 1990 issue of *Discover* magazine, Jared Diamond predicted that the Nile perch will be responsible for more extinctions than any other introduced predator of modern times.

Habitat Destruction. An organism's habitat is where it lives. Many organisms cannot live anywhere else if their natural habitats are destroyed or greatly changed. Human activity causes habitat destruction in numerous ways. When a swamp is drained or filled in so that houses can be built on it, habitat is destroyed (although a new kind of human habitat takes its place). When trees are cut down for timber or to clear land for farming, habitat is destroyed. When a hydroelectric dam controls the flow of water in a river, flooding huge areas of land and draining others, habitats are destroyed. One well-known victim of dam construction is the snail darter, a small fish whose only known habitat, a river in eastern Tennessee, was destroyed by the construction of a dam in the 1970s; the fate of the snail darters, some of which were transplanted to other habitats, is uncertain.

The logging and burning of the tropical rainforests is habitat destruction on a grand, global scale. The biggest conservation controversy in the world today is raging in the rain-forests of the Amazon River basin in South America, where a loose coalition, comprising rubber harvesters who depend on

Habitat destruction caused by acid rain. This denuded forest is near the town of Terplice in Czechoslovakia.

the forests, Indian tribes, and wildlife experts, is pitted against commercial developers, logging and ranching companies, and thousands of land-hungry peasants from other parts of Brazil.

Next to the tropical rainforests, wetlands are the world's most endangered habitats. Wetlands are marshy areas along rivers and lakeshores, at river mouths, and in many places where land and water meet. They support a great number and variety of plants, fish, amphibians, and birds. They are particularly important as nesting grounds and migratory rest stops for hundreds of species of ducks, geese, herons, gulls, and other birds all over the world. But wetlands are fragile environments, easily harmed by waterborne pollutants or by changes in water flow due to irrigation or damming. And because many wetlands are coastal, they are regarded as prime real estate in many areas and are rapidly being filled in for housing and industrial development. Some countries and states have passed laws banning or limiting wetlands development; the conservation efforts of many environmentalists and wildlife biologists are centered on identifying and preserving the wetlands that are most crucial to the survival of the greatest number of shorebirds and other species.

Habitat refers to the type of environment in which a plant or animal can exist, and *range* refers to its actual geographic distribution. Sometimes the two things are the same. Some species' ranges are isolated habitats; when those habitats are destroyed, the species' ranges are gone. For example, Centinela is a single mountain ridge in the South American country of Ecuador. It reaches into the clouds and is separated from other mountain habitats by stretches of tropical lowland. Botanist Alwyn H. Gentry examined the "cloud forest" atop Centinela and identified 38 new species of plants that were endemic to that ridge—that is, they occurred nowhere else. Soon after, the ridge was cleared, and those species perished. No one knows what species of fungi, insects, birds, or mammals might have disappeared along with them. Similarly, the island of Cebu in the Philippines once had 10 endemic species among its bird population. Logging has stripped all of the forest from Cebu, and nine of those species are now extinct. The 10th may survive in zoos and protected parks.

Habitats can also be destroyed by various forms of man-made pollution, such as acid rain, which is caused by the release of sulfur and nitrogen oxides from sources such as motor vehicles, factories, and power plants. Highly acidic precipitation is causing massive global environmental damage, destroying forests (including over half of those in some European countries) and contaminating lakes and streams, often rendering them uninhabitable.

Global warming is also a threat to the habitats of species worldwide. Carbon dioxide and other gases released into the atmosphere—mostly from the burning of fossil fuels such as oil, coal, and natural gas—are trapping heat there, creating a phenomenon known as the greenhouse effect. Although scientists disagree as to whether global warming is already happening, virtually all agree that it will soon do so, increasing average temperatures by 3 to 8 degrees Fahrenheit (1.5 to 4.5 degrees Celsius) by the year 2050. These higher temperatures will disrupt the biosphere in countless ways, including raising sea levels, making plants more susceptible to disease, and altering habitats, thereby threatening numerous species and probably forcing many to migrate in order to survive.

The Domino Effect. All forms of life on earth are

Habitat destruction caused by human expansion. The growth of this residential development will soon eliminate this salt marsh and all the creatures who shelter in it.

interconnected in a myriad of complicated ways that scientists are only beginning to understand. Each ecosystem is a web of interconnections, and a change to one part of the ecosystem is likely to have unforeseen consequences elsewhere. People are constantly making such changes and then being surprised and dismayed at the consequences. The effect is like what happens when standing dominoes are arranged in a row. If the first domino is knocked over, it knocks over the next, which knocks over the next, and so on to the end of the row.

The plight of the hungry puffins is an example of the domino effect. Each year dozens of fishing fleets take enormous quantities of fish from the North Atlantic Ocean. These fish provide a livelihood for many fishermen and food for people in many countries. But the fish are food for other species as well, including the puffin, a glossy black seabird with a large, colorful beak that used to nest by the thousands on the rocky coastal cliffs and islands of the North Atlantic. Puffins are not yet extinct, but their numbers have been sharply reduced by starvation because human fishing has drastically cut their share of the fish. Another example of the domino effect involves the Panama Canal. The digging of the canal in the early 20th century flooded a lake, turning a high ridge into an island called Barro Colorado. It also drove a species called little antbirds into extinction. When the waters began rising around the island, the jaguars and other large predators fled to the mainland. This meant that medium-sized animals such as monkeys flourished on Barro Colorado, unchecked by predators. The monkeys, peccaries (similar to pigs), and coatimundis (similar to raccoons) became so numerous that they ate all the antbirds—and their eggs.

Another kind of domino effect is caused by chemical pollutants such as dichloro-diphenyl-trichloro-ethane (better known as DDT), which began to be used during the 1940s to kill insect pests. This was progress, and yet several decades later it became clear that DDT had worked its way deep into the ecosystem, lingering in food supplies and affecting birds' abilities to reproduce. DDT helped drive the bald eagle and the peregrine falcon almost all the way to extinction. Many countries now have laws against the use of DDT. Those two bird species have even begun to make a comeback. But an even worse threat may be another kind of chemical pollutant, the polychlorinated biphenyls, or PCBs. These chemicals can leak into the environment from insulation or refrigerating units. They cause sterility and birth deformities in animal species. Many fish and bird species in industrially developed nations are severely threatened by PCBs.

Plastic trash also has a destructive effect on many species. The person who invented those handy plastic holders for six-packs of beer and soft drink cans did not *mean* to kill gulls, seals, and turtles. He or she was only looking for a cheap, convenient way to package consumer goods. Yet each year in Alaska's Pribilof Islands alone, 30,000 fur seals die by becoming entangled in plastic fishing lines or six-pack rings. Discarded plastics also kill as many as 70,000 other marine mammals and 2 million seabirds yearly, according to the World Resources Institute.

Overhunting. In addition to activities that indirectly threaten species, such as habitat destruction and introduction of new predators, humans eliminate other life-forms through a variety of direct actions that can be grouped together under the label "overhunting." One such action is hunting for food. A few societies, such as the whale-hunting native peoples of Greenland and northern Canada and certain forest tribes of Borneo and the Amazon region, still live in part by hunting. A much greater percentage of all hunting, however, is done for commercial purposes, such as by Japanese fleets that fish for whales in spite of international treaties calling for an end to commercial whale hunting.

Animals are also hunted for sport. Most nations have laws that govern what species can be hunted and how many animals can be killed. Wildlife is an economic resource, and countries that permit big-game hunting are usually careful to preserve that resource. One country's income, however, may be another

continued on page 73

A pair of penguins scurry across a pile of garbage left by scientists near Esperanza Station, Antarctica. Such habitat destruction is a major cause of species extinction. The following pages show a number of the planet's most endangered species and the environmental destruction with which they must cope.

Amazon rainforest before, during, and after its destruction by slash-and-burn clearing. Harvard biologist E. O. Wilson believes that such destruction renders between 4,000 and 6,000 species extinct every year.

The African elephant is one of the most endangered species in the world today. In spite of laws protecting the animal, it is slaughtered in great numbers for its ivory tusks.

The ocelot, a tree-climbing cat found in tropical forests. All such cats—leopards, pumas, jaguars, and tigers—are hunted for their colorful skins and are becoming rarer.

A gibbon rests in the treetops as it forages for food. As the rainforests of the world shrink, these primates lose their habitat.

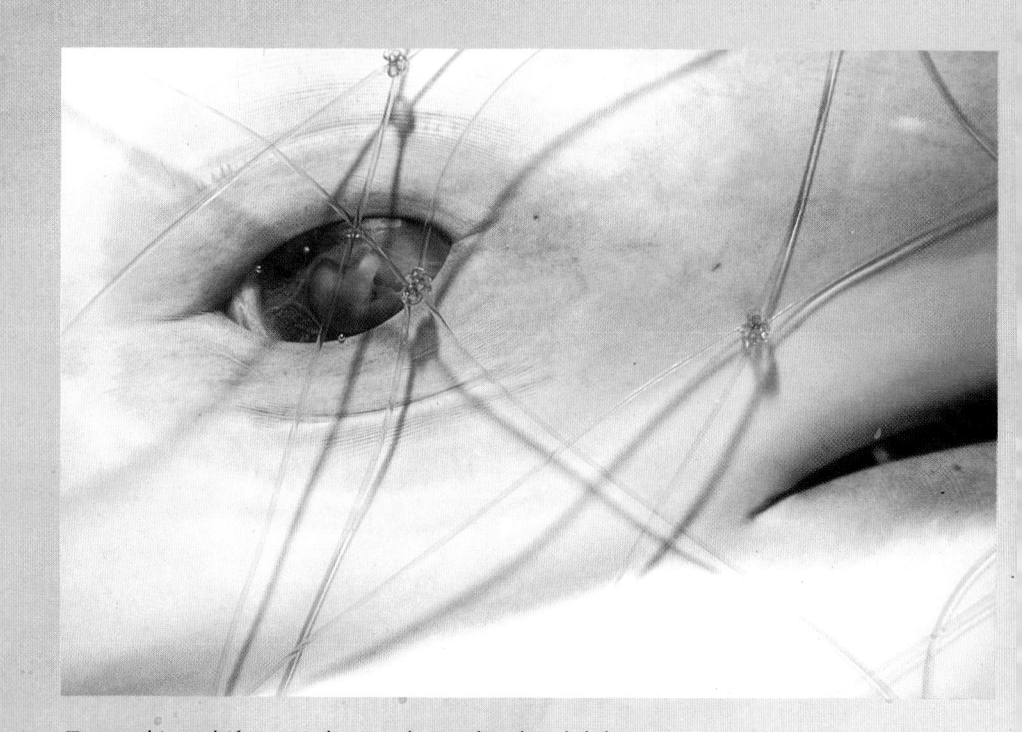

Trapped in a drift net in the North Pacific, this dolphin will die even though it has no commercial value to the fishermen who have ensnared it.

This California condor was raised to adulthood in captivity. No California condors remain in the wild.

Two tropical tree frogs in different color phases. Recently scientists have noted a worldwide decline in populations of frogs and other amphibians. Although the reason is unknown, some form of air or water pollution is suspected.

Unlike the creatures shown on previous pages, which still have a chance to survive if human beings care enough, the brontosaurus became extinct about 140 million years ago. The dying off of these great reptiles left room in the environment for mammals to evolve to larger sizes.

continued from page 64

country's outrage. In 1989, the Asian nation of Mongolia charged three hunters $16,000 each for permission to shoot snow leopards, even though these cats are an endangered species. (Only about 5,000 or so snow leopards are thought to survive. They are protected by law from hunting throughout their ranges in Nepal and Tibet, but poaching is common.) Wildlife lovers around the world have condemned Mongolia for letting snow leopards be hunted, but the Mongolian government argues that fees from carefully controlled hunting will help pay for conservation programs that will benefit all of the country's wildlife. Only about 300 foreign hunters visit Mongolia each year, but their sport is an expensive one. They spend a total of about $2 million for the increasingly rare chance to bag a large wild animal such as the snow leopard or the argali sheep.

Pest control is another reason people kill animals and ultimately whole species. The Tasmanian wolf was a striped, wolflike marsupial native to the island of Tasmania, off the south coast of Australia. During the 19th century, European settlers who wanted to raise sheep on Tasmania killed as many Tasmanian wolves as they could find. The species has been thought to be extinct since about 1930, although every now and then the tantalizing rumor of a wolf sighting drifts out of the Tasmanian backwoods. True wolves have also been shot as pests by farmers and ranchers; the once-numerous North American gray wolf is now endangered as a result.

In the 1930s and 1940s, farmers on the Great Plains of the west central United States fought a bitter war with the prairie dog, a large ground squirrel that lives in big colonies in underground burrows. Prairie dogs were considered destructive and useless pests and were poisoned and shot by the hundreds of

The peregrine falcon was nearly exterminated by illegal hunting and the spraying of DDT.

thousands. There are very few of them left today. And as a result, there are even fewer black-footed ferrets. In a perfect example of the domino effect combined with overhunting, the attack on the prairie dogs almost wiped out the black-footed ferret, a weasel-like carnivore that lives in abandoned prairie dog burrows and eats nothing but prairie dogs. The black-footed ferret is one of the rarest North American mammals. Only a single protected colony, with about 50 or 60 members, now remains. New laws have been made to protect the species, but it may be headed for extinction anyway. Once a species' numbers are that small, biologists have learned, recovery is very far from a sure thing. And human intervention—whether direct or indirect, deliberate or accidental—has so far killed many more species than it has saved.

This poacher in northern Peru has captured several rare parrots, which will be illegally shipped to unscrupulous pet dealers in the United States and Europe.

chapter 5

SPECIES FOR SALE

The rhinoceros is a large animal, weighing several tons. But rhinos—which are protected by law in the African and Asian countries where they live—are not sought for their meat. They are, however, eagerly and rapaciously hunted for the horns they bear on their snouts or foreheads. The rhino poachers usually use high-powered rifles or even machine guns. Sometimes, to save ammunition, they just wound the rhino, remove its horn and part of its face with a chain saw, and leave it to bleed to death. The horn, which is made of a hardened material similar to hair or fingernails, is thought by many Asian people to be an effective medicine or a sexual stimulant; this persistent but unfounded belief makes powdered rhino horn worth its weight in gold in some marketplaces. Because of relentless poaching, there were fewer than 11,000 rhinos left in the world in 1990, down from about 75,000 in 1970. "No other animal family has been as devastated by trade," says Sarah Fitzgerald in *International Wildlife Trade: Whose Business Is It?* If they keep killing the rhinos at the current rate, the poachers may soon put themselves out of business. That will not help the rhinos, of course.

This beautifully patterned leopard skin will be sold to make someone an expensive and fashionable fur coat.

Rhinoceroses are not the only creatures that are hunted for reasons that have nothing to do with food, sport, or pest control. Many species of animals and plants—including many that are known to be threatened or endangered—are hunted, gathered, poached, or otherwise harvested for a booming international industry. That industry is the trade in wildlife products, which is worth at least $5 billion each year for animals and animal products alone, according to the World Wildlife Fund. Some transactions involving wildlife are legal; others are illegal. According to conservationists, some of the legal transactions should be illegal because they threaten the survival of species or ecosystems.

Elephants are hunted for their ivory. Snakes and lizards are hunted for their skins, which are often made into expensive cowboy boots and pocketbooks. Turtles are hunted for their shells, which are carved into combs and ornaments. Wildcats, such as the African leopard, the South American jaguar, and the central Asian snow leopard, are hunted for their luxuriously soft, beautifully patterned pelts, which are made into rugs, wall ornaments, and fur coats. (In parts of Europe and North America, ecological awareness is slowly making it unfashionable to wear fur. Some of the great cats may yet be saved from overhunting, although they still face the problem of habitat destruction because many of them are rainforest dwellers.) Chimpanzees and monkeys are trapped and sold as pets or for scientific and medical research. European nations import 12,000 or so hummingbirds from South America each year; some of the birds are sold as pets, and the rest are killed so that their shiny, brilliantly colored feathers can be made into jewelry. Parrots account for a large portion of the wildlife trade. The United States is the biggest importer of parrots, taking in more than 300,000 of these colorful, sociable birds each year from Latin America, Africa, and Asia. Wildlife experts estimate that as many as one-third of these birds are illegal imports, either because they have been poached and smuggled out of countries where they are protected by law or because U.S. law does not permit them to enter the United States.

The wildlife trade embraces all types of organisms. Tropical fish are gathered from coral reefs, rivers, and lakes and sold to aquarium owners worldwide. One problem with this business is that some of the fish are endangered species; another problem is that some fishermen in the Philippines and other countries use the poison cyanide to stun and catch the fish. Over time, this practice kills the reefs and *all* the species that inhabit them. Reefs are sensitively balanced ecosystems that can easily be disrupted. The harvesting of coral for jewelry making and for use as a raw material in road building and construction also threatens the world's coral reefs, which grow very slowly.

Even insects play a part in the international wildlife trade. Certain butterflies and beetles are prized for their vividly colored wings or metallic-looking shells, which are made into novelty jewelry. The red-kneed tarantula, a poisonous spider from western Mexico, is a popular pet. About 30,000 of them are sold each year in the United States, Japan, and Great Britain, although the species cannot legally be exported from Mexico.

THE PLANT AND TIMBER TRADE

Animals, birds, fish, and insects are only part of the picture. Plants of many sorts are also very marketable. Orchids are among the most complex and beautiful of the world's flowering plants, and they have long been highly prized by collectors, who buy, sell, or trade about 3 million of them worldwide each year. The World Wildlife Fund says that at least one-sixth of all these transactions involve wild orchids, not cultivated or greenhouse stock. Japan imports about 60% of all imported orchids. The United States imports about 700,000 orchids yearly; half of these are wild. The rivalry among collectors, and their desire for ever rarer species, have driven the prices of some exotic specimens past $1,500 per flower. For sums like that, many orchid hunters are more than willing to uproot rare or fragile species to supply the collectors. A particularly rare species, for example, was discovered on a single hillside in China in 1982; specimens were being sold in Japan, the United States, Great Britain, and Taiwan the following year.

Another star of the plant trade is the cactus. Most of the rarest and most desirable cacti come from Mexico, and many of them are endangered species. Nonetheless, at least 800,000 wild cacti are exported to the United States alone each year, many of them illegally. Japan, the Netherlands, Belgium, and Germany are the other major importers of cacti from Mexico and Central and South America. A university in Ciudad Victoria, Mexico, is trying to reverse the flow of cacti across the border. The border patrols seize illegal shipments of cacti and turn them over to the school, which operates a plant nursery for the collection and breeding of cacti native to Mexico's Sonoran Desert. To work in the nursery, the university hires the same local people who once gathered wild cacti for smugglers and collectors, giving them a chance to help the cacti survive instead of wiping them out.

The trade in tropical timber overshadows the problems raised by orchids and cacti. The international tropical timber trade is worth $7 to $8 billion each year, mostly in wood from Asian forests. Some logging does take place in the rainforests of Central and South America, but the greater part of the rainforest destruction there is caused by fires that are set to burn off the vegetation so that the land can be farmed—slash-and-burn agriculture, as it is called. In Southeast Asia and the Pacific, however, the rainforests are being chewed up by logging companies and spit out in the form of hastily processed lumber. Much of this lumber is cheap plywood that is purchased by Japan. The biggest use the Japanese make of it is in throwaway forms for molding concrete in construction projects.

Logging has stripped vast tracts of forest from the Philippines, Thailand, Indonesia, and Papua New Guinea. Now the island of Borneo, which contains some of the oldest rainforests on earth, is under assault. Sarawak and Sabah, two states on Borneo that belong to the nation of Malaysia, are the hardest hit, supplying about 90% of Japan's lumber. In mid-1989, a Malaysian forestry expert estimated that those two states would be deforested within seven years. The Penan, a tribal people native to the forests of Sarawak, are trying to keep the loggers out with blockades and protests, but so far they have had little success.

WILDLIFE ECONOMICS

The tropical timber business is not the only area of the international wildlife trade in which Japan makes a poor showing. For many years, Japan has been one of the largest world markets for exotic wildlife products. Japanese craftsmen have carved countless thousands of *hanko,* or signature seals, from elephant ivory, importing 135,000 tusks in 1983 and 1984 alone for that purpose, and they have fashioned ornamental wedding combs from the shells of endangered hawksbill turtles. Japan is one of the few countries in the world in which whale meat can be found on restaurant menus. But Japan's biggest sin, in the eyes of many international conservationists, is its use of drift nets for fishing in the Pacific Ocean. Drift nets are huge nylon webs, up to 40 miles (64 kilometers) long. Thousands of miles of these nets are set up in the sea to trap tuna and squid by entanglement. Other marine species, however, are also trapped in the nets. Victims include whales, dolphins, seals, sea turtles, and birds. Roger McManus of the Center for Marine Conservation says that their use of drift nets makes the Japanese "environmental terrorists." Fishing fleets from other countries, including the United States, also use drift nets; however, only fleets from Japan, South Korea, and Taiwan still practice large-scale, high-seas drift netting.

In the late 1980s, Japan appeared to be responding to worldwide pressure to improve its environmental manners. Although tropical deforestation in Asia and drift-net fishing continue, the Japanese have banned the import of some wildlife products and limited imports of others. They will no longer trade in green sea turtles, musk deer, or monitor lizards, all of which are endangered species. They have agreed to comply with an international ban on trade in ivory, and whaling has been

Turtle soup has its price, as shown by this pile of sea-turtle shells discarded by a slaughterhouse in Oaxaca, Mexico.

significantly reduced, although not eliminated. Japan and several other nations have circumvented the International Whaling Commission's ban on commercial whaling, begun in 1986, by killing thousands of these animals in the name of "scientific research," according to the World Wildlife Fund.

No one nation is to blame for the international market in endangered species or wildlife products. Many of the poorer nations of the developing world have environments that seem exotic to the developed world: tropical rainforests, deserts, coral reefs, and all the rich and diverse plant and animal life that inhabit them. At the same time, many of the people who live in these countries face a daily struggle just to live. A poacher who brings down an elephant or a rhino may earn a year's worth of wages with a single squeeze of the trigger; a farmer who traps rare parrots and sells them to a smuggler may find it difficult to worry about the long-term survival of a species when his family's short-term survival is at stake.

Although many wildlife experts and conservation groups would like to see plants and animals and their habitats preserved for their own sake, with no human interference or exploitation, "pure" preservation of this sort is increasingly hard to justify in countries with growing populations and little money. By the 1990s, most conservationists have realized that species preservation cannot always be a purely ethical or scientific matter—in many cases, in order for governments and citizens to support preservation, it must also make economic sense. Governments and conservation groups are therefore trying to help people in developing nations use their resources, including their wildlife, in ways that will bring in money without destroying the environment or driving species to extinction. One such program in Peru involves the wild vicuña, a grazing animal of the high Andes Mountains that has long been prized for its fine, silky wool. Once the vicuña was threatened with extinction by overhunting. Today the local Andean Indians are permitted to capture vicuñas and shear their wool, but only during certain seasons and under government control. The Indians can then use the wool in a local textile industry, making traditional cloth and crafts for export. Under this system, the animals contribute to the local economy but are protected from overhunting.

Using wildlife in a controlled manner for economic purposes is called *sustainable use* or *sustainable development.* Many conservationists see sustainable use as the only practical hope for some species. In Thailand and Papua New Guinea, some villages are trying to raise crocodiles and butterflies commercially, hoping that "ranching" can provide products for international trade without diminishing the number of wild crocs and butterflies. A U.S. ice cream company buys nuts from South American rainforest dwellers who gather the nuts from the forest floor without harming the trees—although the other species that eat the nuts may not benefit in the long run.

Through sustainable development projects, wild species and natural environments may be able to pay their way in a world of ever more crowded and hungry humans. Another source of income from wild habitats is a fast-growing industry called ecological tourism, or ecotourism. As wildlife and pristine natural environments become rarer, more and more people are eager to see them. And when tourists visit a country to see its wildlife or national parks, the money they spend on hotels, fees, purchases, and services enriches that country's economy. For example, in Kenya—where game wardens have orders to shoot poachers on

A dolphin entangled in a nylon drift net. Designed to catch tuna and squid, these nets, which can be up to 40 miles long, ensnare and kill many other species.

sight—tourism is the country's biggest source of income. Kenya earns about $400 million from a total of more than 700,000 tourists each year. Most of those tourists come to see the country's wildlife, including its 20,000 elephants. Perez Olindo of the African Wildlife Foundation in Nairobi, Kenya, figures that each elephant is therefore responsible for $20,000 of income; this is about 10 times the black-market value of its tusks. And the elephants will attract tourists year after year—whereas the tusks can be harvested only once.

If the developed nations of the industrial world are serious about halting the headlong slide toward extinction, they are going to have to make preservation economically worthwhile for people in less developed countries, perhaps by forgiving foreign debts in exchange for improved conservation measures (such "debt-for-nature" swaps have already taken place in several countries). They are also going to have to set an example at home. For instance, many Americans are quick to criticize Brazil for allowing its tropical forests to be ravaged by slash-and-burn clearing. But most of the cleared forest land is turned into cattle pastures, and most of the beef that is produced is sold to fast-food companies in the United States. As Christopher Lampton writes in his book *Endangered Species*, "The most prolific natural environment on earth is being traded for cheap hamburgers."

It will do very little good for the people of Europe and North America to cry out in alarm at the ruin of natural resources in the Third World as long as their purchases of wildlife products encourage further destruction. Germany has long been one of the biggest markets for the furs of leopards and other endangered great cats; the United States is a principal market for reptile skins and exotic pets; France has been harshly criticized by conservationists for failing to control the traffic in endangered wildlife that flows through French Guiana, a French territory in South America. These and the other developed countries have the power to curb the trade in wildlife and possibly to save many species of animals and plants from extinction, if their governments act together and act now.

This Tanzanian ivory carver is turning an animal tusk into a work of art for export. In 1988 the government of Tanzania outlawed all trade in ivory.

chapter 6

PRESERVATION AND PROTECTION

Why should species be preserved? Should preservation stand in the way of human expansion? Should the survival of a wild animal outweigh a family's need to eat? Will the world really be poorer if the endangered Corsican swallowtail butterfly vanishes from its Mediterranean home or if the Columbian tiger beetle of the central United States becomes extinct?

These are reasonable questions. Conservationists and a growing body of ordinary citizens around the world feel that human beings are custodians of the natural world and have an inherent responsibility to protect other forms of life rather than exterminate them. These people believe that the death of each species diminishes the beauty and richness of life and impoverishes the heritage of future generations. But many others question the need to protect wild plants and animals, especially when that protection conflicts with human needs and desires. Even many of those who approve of efforts to save the pandas and elephants wonder why they should be concerned about the fate of an obscure insect or a tiny tropical flower that no one but a few scientists will ever see.

One argument against conservation is that extinction is part of evolution, part of the history of life. After all, extinction has happened before, and on a large scale. But today's mass extinction is different. It is the first mass extinction that has been caused by the growth and activity of a single species, and it is the first that could be controlled or prevented. For this reason alone, many scientists and conservationists argue, the current massacre of species should not be compared to the earth's previous episodes of mass extinction. They also warn that the planet's present *biodiversity*—that is, the number and variety of its species, including *Homo sapiens*—evolved into a harmonious and balanced system over millions of years and that all species may be interrelated in complex, unknown, and vitally important ways. Chipping away at biodiversity with a species here and a species there may weaken the entire biosphere until, at some critical point, *all* species are threatened. But there are other, more direct arguments for preserving biodiversity. Humanity benefits from wild species in a number of very material ways.

THE BENEFITS OF BIODIVERSITY

A great deal of habitat destruction, particularly deforestation, takes place when land is cleared for farming. No one would argue that food production is not important; indeed, it gains importance daily as the world's population grows larger and hungrier. Yet tropical rainforest soil is poorly suited for agriculture and generally does not produce good crops for more than a year or two. Wild habitats, however, may contain plants that could

These huge logs from the rainforest of Southeast Asia are being prepared for transport to the lumber mill. The demand of the industrialized nations for wood destroys an enormous amount of tropical wildlife habitat.

become useful food crops. Biologists estimate that about 75,000 plant species have edible parts, but only about 7,000 have been used for food during human history. Most agriculture today depends on about 30 species, such as wheat and rice. The wilderness may contain food species that are equal or superior to these. One example is the winged bean plant of New Guinea. According to biologist E. O. Wilson, it grows rapidly to a height of 15 feet (4.57 meters), is entirely edible, and has the same nutritional value as the soybean. This plant could help feed the world—or it could become extinct before its potential is realized.

Wild plants are also necessary to keep cultivated food species healthy. Species bred in controlled conditions over long periods of time—which includes all food plants—can suffer from what is called genetic erosion, a progressive weakening of the species that makes it less productive or leaves it vulnerable to disease. When this happens to domestic plants, they are crossbred with their wild relatives. This crossbreeding is called *hybridization*, and it brings strong new genetic material into the strain. But hybridization depends upon the survival of such hardy wild species as teosinte, a wild relative of corn that grows in Mexico. Agricultural scientists claim that if teosinte becomes extinct, the many varieties of corn that are grown by the world's farmers will eventually be threatened.

Recent advances in genetics may soon allow people to profit even more from biodiversity. Genetic engineers are learning how to mix and match genes from closely related species. Experts claim that they can draw upon the genetic wealth of wild species to make food crops more productive or to create new strains that are resistant to heat, drought, frost, disease, and insect pests.

Medicine is another area in which people reap direct benefits from the wild. Nearly 25% of all prescription medicines used in the United States contain ingredients that were originally obtained from wild plants; some 40 or so plants provide most of these medical substances. The opium poppy provides the painkillers codeine and morphine (as well as the illegal drugs opium and heroin). The cinchona tree provides quinine, a drug used to treat malaria and other tropical diseases. The foxglove provides digitalis, which is used to treat heart disease. The Pacific yew—a tree that environmentalists argue should be listed as a threatened species—yields a promising new drug used to treat several forms of cancer.

The island of Madagascar is particularly rich in plants with medicinal value. The haronga plant provides a medicine used to treat stomachaches; a Madagascan weed is the source of a drug that helps skin wounds heal; another Madagascan plant is being investigated as a possible treatment for bubonic plague, which has killed millions of people in periodic epidemics throughout history. The best-known Madagascan medicinal plant is the rosy periwinkle. It produces two chemicals that are used in the treatment of childhood leukemia and Hodgkin's disease. The income from these substances is about $100 million per year. Five close relatives of the rosy periwinkle also grow in Madagascar, and none has yet been tested for medical use. One or more of them may contain lifesaving chemicals. At least one of them is severely endangered by habitat destruction.

Wild habitats around the world—particularly tropical rainforests—may contain cures for cancer, AIDS, and a host of other diseases. At a 1988 conference on the environmental crisis hosted by *Time* magazine, biologist Daniel Janzen of the University of Pennsylvania said, "I know of three plants with the potential to treat AIDS. One grows in an Australian rain forest, one in Panama, and one in Costa Rica." Janzen says that the wholesale destruction of species before they are studied or even recognized is "as though the nations of the world had decided to burn their libraries without bothering to see what is in them."

CONSERVATION ORGANIZATIONS AND LAWS

The best hope for the world's endangered species lies in the efforts of a host of conservation organizations and agencies. Some of them are sponsored by governments; some are private. Some are international in scope; some are local and focused on particular sites or species. Each is working in its own way to save plants and animals from extinction.

The wildlife conservation movement got started in Europe and North America in the 19th century, when people began to be

continued on page 96

CONSERVATION CONTROVERSY

A battle is raging over the old-growth cedar, spruce, and hemlock forests of Washington and Oregon in the Pacific Northwest. This is the habitat of the northern spotted owl, and it is under heavy assault by the logging industry. It is thought that only about 3,000 spotted owls remain. In 1987 several conservation groups asked the U.S. Fish and Wildlife Service (USFWS) to place the spotted owl on the endangered species list; the USFWS refused. The conservationists went to court. In 1988 a federal district court judge declared that the USFWS's refusal had been "contrary to law." In 1990 the conservationists were still fighting to get the spotted owl on the list. If this owl is named an endangered species, the provisions of the Endangered Species Act that deal with habitat protection will come into play, and logging will be sharply affected throughout the bird's range.

The movement to save the northern spotted owl is opposed by the logging industry, which claims that the conservationists are using the owl as a way to protect the forests. Whole towns in Washington are dependent upon logging for their income, and many people are angry that the welfare of an obscure bird may be placed above their welfare and that of their families. However, those who favor preservation claim that reckless logging practices threaten the industry and will put loggers out of work before long anyway and that controlled logging of individual trees, as opposed to clear-cutting of whole forests, will be to the advantage of both the spotted owls and the loggers. As resources such as forests grow ever more scarce, conflicts of this kind are bound to become more frequent, and the economic costs of protecting the environment, in terms of threatened industries and jobs, is bound to rise. No one can predict the long-term effects of the loss of an individual species. The only certainty is that although few people will ever see a northern spotted owl in the wild, a growing number of people on both sides of the conflict care passionately about its fate.

The fate of the northern spotted owl turns on the outcome of a dispute between conservationists and the logging industry over the use of the Pacific Northwest's forests.

continued from page 93

alarmed and outraged by the large-scale slaughter of birds for feathers that were used in women's hats. A number of laws and treaties to protect birds—and other creatures such as fur seals—came into existence between the 1870s and the 1920s. From that time on, the wildlife preservation movement slowly gained international momentum as people began to recognize that whole environments and groups of species could be threatened with extinction.

The environmental movement came of age in the 1970s, and concerns about extinction grew more pressing at that time. In 1973, the International Union for the Conservation of Nature and Natural Resources (IUCN) met to draw up the single most important international wildlife agreement yet created. It is called the Convention on International Trade in Endangered Species of Wild Fauna and Flora, usually shortened to CITES. When the final draft of CITES was passed in 1975, 85 nations signed it. By 1990, 20 more had signed, for a total of 105 signatory nations. The purpose of CITES is to promote international conservation of seriously endangered species while allowing controlled trade in wildlife or wildlife products from species that are not endangered. The treaty includes three appendices, or lists. Appendix I lists more than 600 species of plants and animals that are considered endangered. Trade in these species is prohibited, except in strictly limited cases for research purposes. Appendix II lists more than 2,300 animal species and more than 24,000 plant species that may be traded only if such trade is legal in their countries of origin. These species are monitored by scientists because their numbers may be declining; some conservationists regard Appendix II as a "waiting list" for Appendix I. Appendix III is a list of species that are protected by their countries of origin. Any nation that has signed the CITES treaty may place any plant or animal on Appendix III, which means that it cannot be traded without legally issued export permits.

CITES was a landmark in wildlife protection. Yet the treaty has a large loophole. In order to get nations to sign it, the IUCN had to include a clause that allows any nation to take a reservation on any species—that is, to make that species exempt from protection. The reservation provision has allowed nations that are members of CITES to trade openly in endangered species; for example, Japan has taken reservations on more than a dozen endangered species, including several kinds of whale. Conservation efforts in many countries are aimed at getting those nations to drop their reservations.

Each nation enforces CITES with its own laws and enforcement agencies. The United States supports CITES with the Endangered Species Act (ESA) of 1973, which makes it illegal for anyone in the United States to trade in species listed by CITES without the proper permits. The task of interpreting and enforcing the ESA falls to the U.S. Fish and Wildlife Service (USFWS), a division of the Department of the Interior. The USFWS periodically publishes a current list of endangered or threatened species. Under the ESA, it is illegal for a U.S. citizen to kill, trap, gather, capture, trade, or even chase any species on that list. In

The great saguaro cactus grows taller than a human being. It is protected by federal law, but each plant may be worth up to $15,000 on the black market.

addition, most individual states have their own wildlife or fish and game departments, and a number of state laws reinforce the ESA. In Arizona, for example, the saguaro cactus is protected by both federal and state law. Yet the fact that these tall cacti are worth up to $15,000 each on the cactus black market lures illegal collectors. A 4-year undercover investigation into a saguaro-trading ring resulted in the arrest of 21 people in early 1990.

Enforcement of the ESA has generally proved difficult, however. A 1990 internal investigation by the Department of the Interior concluded that the USFWS's program to protect endangered species was poorly managed and vastly underfunded. Hundreds—perhaps thousands—of species that should be listed as endangered are not, and many of those that are listed have not received adequate protection. Some species have even become extinct without ever having received protected status.

The United States has several other laws that regulate wildlife trade. The most important of these are the Marine Mammal Protection Act, which outlaws trade in sea mammals, such as otters and walruses; the Migratory Bird Treaty Act, which places limits on trade in wild birds native to the United States; and the Lacey Act, which supports other countries' conservation efforts by making it illegal for a U.S. citizen to import animals or animal products that were obtained or exported in violation of the laws of their country of origin. This means that an American may not buy *any* animal that is illegally harvested in or smuggled out of its own country.

In some cases, individual enforcement laws are even stricter than the CITES treaty itself. The 12 nations that form the European Community (EC) have a unified wildlife policy that treats some Appendix II species as if they were Appendix I species, giving them extra protection. Yet some of the EC countries—notably Germany, France, Spain, and Italy—are among the world's largest consumers of wildlife products. Conservationists hope that stricter enforcement of the EC policy will curb wildlife imports into these countries.

Treaties and laws are a vital part of conservation, but private organizations are also extremely important; in fact, the pressure exerted by these organizations creates many of the treaties and laws. Among the largest and most active wildlife conservation groups are the World Wildlife Fund, which serves as an international clearinghouse of information, a project organizer, and a major fund-raiser; the Nature Conservancy, which buys up and preserves tracts of endangered habitats, such as wetlands and rainforest; the Sierra Club, which was founded by the American naturalist John Muir; the National Audubon Society, which started as a birdwatchers' organization but has branched out into many kinds of conservation work; and Greenpeace, whose ecological activists call public attention to a variety of environmental issues.

These groups and government agencies around the world are working to halt practices that threaten wildlife and to start projects that may help. For example, in 1989 the World Wildlife Fund drew up a plan for saving the elephants in the African nations of Kenya, Tanzania, and Zaire. The program calls for co-ordination among these governments and their agencies, as well as a handful of private conservation groups. If it is accepted, it could serve as a model for other global action plans, ensuring that the most efficient possible use is made of the money and energy that individuals and governments give to endangered species.

A silverback male mountain gorilla. Only a handful of families still survive in protected areas of Rwanda, in central Africa.

chapter 7

ON THE BRINK OF EXTINCTION

All over the world, species are in big trouble. On the Atlantic coast of Brazil, which was once covered with tropical forest but has been almost completely cleared for development, the golden lion tamarin hovers on the edge of extinction. The tamarin is a shy, elusive creature like a small monkey with a ruff of golden fur. No one knows how many remain in the wild; some experts estimate their numbers at 100. In the highlands of central Africa, 500 or so mountain gorillas are sheltered in wildlife parks. The parks must be patrolled by armed rangers to prevent poaching and the encroachment of neighboring farmers. Across the Indian Ocean in Borneo and Sumatra, the orangutans, cousins of the gorillas, are similarly imperiled by poaching and habitat destruction. The tamarin, the gorilla, and the orangutan are primates, members of the same order of animals to which human beings belong; they are among humankind's closest relatives. That relationship has not spared them from the threat of extinction at human hands, however. Other mammals, birds, reptiles, fish, insects, and plants have received no more consideration—much less, in many cases.

In early 1990, there were small signs of hope, indications that the tide may be turning for some species. Canadian wildlife officials and conservationists tried to cut down poaching of the Canadian black bear by tightening controls on the sale of wild animal parts (the gall bladder of the bear, like the rhino's horn, is mistakenly believed by some people to have medicinal or sexually stimulating properties). Sudan, a large country in north-central Africa, banned the hunting, killing, and capture of *all* mammals, birds, and reptiles until a complete wildlife survey could be carried out and a long-term plan for wildlife protection developed. Peru banned the export of orchids and now requires a legal export permit for any plant or animal that is shipped out of the country, even if the species is not listed by CITES. In the United States, a museum official was sentenced to 18 months in prison for his involvement in a ring that smuggled endangered species of rattlesnakes and other reptiles into the country.

A baby orangutan in the arms of its mother. The orangutan is one of humankind's closest relatives; like most primates, it is endangered.

Malaysia extended a ban on the export of two rare species of macaques, members of the monkey family, although it still permits the macaques to be hunted for food within the country. Government authorities in Belgium broke up a large orchid-smuggling ring and seized more than 1,000 orchids, including some wild species listed on CITES Appendix I.

Every effort that is made to save individual species is worthwhile. Yet more and more people are realizing that particular species are no longer the major issue. Instead, habitat destruction and human overpopulation are breaking down whole habitats and ecosystems, jeopardizing entire networks of species large and small. As the 1980s drew to a close, scientists were trying to educate the public about the crisis in biodiversity.

Harvard's E. O. Wilson calls the current crisis "the death of birth." He points out that humanity is not merely killing particular species by the score but is dismantling the ecosystems that would, over many generations, produce new species. The present generation is doing more than just tampering with the present moment in geologic and biological time; it may be stopping the clock forever for many categories of life. Norman Myers, a British ecologist, has called the accelerating avalanche of extinctions "the greatest single setback to life's abundance and diversity since the first flickerings of life almost 4 billion years ago."

WHO GETS INTO THE ARK?

Faced with the ever-mounting biodiversity crisis, scientists are trying to develop a plan that will help them use the available time and money to the best effect. In the process, they are realizing that some painful choices will have to be made. Three

continued on page 106

In his 1989 book, *The End of Nature*, Bill McKibben made a claim that many people found deeply disturbing. He suggested that nature no longer exists in the same way that it has existed throughout history. Human cultures have always recognized the natural world as larger and more powerful than the human race, as something separate from man and existing on a grander scale. Today, McKibben says, the natural world is threatened with outright destruction by *Homo sapiens*. Wild environments and creatures cannot survive without human protection. From being something immense and all-embracing, nature has been reduced to a set of carefully managed wilderness areas.

For many species, nature has already "ended." These species can no longer live in the wild, mostly because their habitats have been destroyed. For these creatures—and their number increases yearly—the world's zoos are a last refuge.

Until recently, zoos were little more than showplaces of exotic animals. By the 1980s, however, most of the world's large zoos had acquired a new role as guardians of the biodiversity that is rapidly vanishing from the wild. No longer does every zoo strive to have one animal of every species, all lined up in rows of cages. Instead, zoos try to re-create habitats or ecosystems, such as stretches of African plain or small tropical rainforests, in which a number of species can live together in conditions not far removed from those that once existed in their natural homes. Zoos have also become important centers of biological and ecological research, with scientists of all sorts on their staff.

Perhaps the most important role that zoos play in species preservation, however, is that of captive breeding. Zoos maintain detailed data bases, which have been compared to dating services for animals. To avoid genetic erosion caused by inbreeding, zoos carefully swap animals for breeding. Using a new technique called DNA fingerprinting, zoo biologists can find the best potential mates for members of severely endangered species, such as the California condor, which now exists only in captivity. And zoos are experimenting with techniques such as test-tube fertilization, freezing sperm and eggs for breeding with future generations, and surrogate mothering in attempts to save species such as the Siberian tiger, the Florida panther, and the Suni antelope. The time may not be far off when zoos are much more than places for people to look at and learn about the world's animals—they may become the animals' sole islands of survival in an ocean of habitat destruction.

This tiger cub was born in a captive breeding program at the Henry Doorly Zoo in Omaha, Nebraska. All such large cats are hunted for their colorful skins; breeding programs offer some hope that these animals can be pulled back from the brink of extinction.

continued from page 103

thousand scientists attended a meeting on biodiversity sponsored by the American Institute of Biological Sciences in August 1988. There they discussed proposals for a quick survey of selected sites on the planet to identify regions of especially high biodiversity. Thomas Lovejoy of the Smithsonian Institution suggested that scientists around the world might collaborate on a speedy study of butterflies, woody plants, birds, freshwater fish, and other vertebrates in several hundred sites. The results of such a survey would tell conservationists where to establish the most urgently needed wildlife reserves. To biologists who had favored the idea of a careful, systematic inventory of all of the world's species, Lovejoy's suggestion was a departure from normal scientific procedures. But many of them agreed that it had merit. E. O. Wilson said that the quick survey would be "far better than doing nothing, and better than the haphazard way we have been doing things."

As of 1990, no formal plan for a global survey had been adopted by the Smithsonian, but scientists from many institutions are working together on smaller surveys and sharing their research findings with the goal of piecing together a rough-and-ready biodiversity atlas. Many scientists have already developed their own lists of ecological trouble spots. A typical list is that of Norman Myers, who says that the world's most endangered rainforest regions are western Colombia, the plateau uplands of the western Amazon River basin, the Atlantic coast of Brazil, the island of Madagascar (where 90% of the original vegetation has been destroyed), the foothills of the eastern Himalaya Mountains, the Philippines, Malaysia, northwestern Borneo, Australia's Queensland state, and the western Pacific island of New Caledonia.

Thomas Lovejoy of the Smithsonian Institution. Intimately involved in the struggle to save the rainforest, Lovejoy suggested in 1988 that scientists conduct a global survey to identify the most endangered species and habitats.

Although the scientific community is firm in its belief that the extinction crisis is real and getting worse, it is far from united on the best course of action. One point of view is that of James Brown of the University of New Mexico, who has suggested that not all species need to be saved. Rather than concentrating their efforts on species preservation and the establishment of wildlife reserves, says Brown, scientists and conservationists should push for national and even international land-use planning that would control development in what he calls the "semi-natural matrix," the 85% or so of the earth's land that is neither farmland nor city.

Brown and like-minded scientists are suggesting an approach similar to what doctors call *triage*. Triage means that in an emergency situation with limited medical resources, doctors quickly evaluate each patient and then work on those patients who have the best chance to pull through. They do not try to save the patients who are likely to die whether they receive treatment or not. Applied to biology, triage would mean that the conservation effort would be focused on species that have a good chance of surviving with assistance. Species that are unlikely to survive even with human help would be left to fend for themselves.

Triage is a painful reality in some medical situations. Many scientists find it both difficult and distasteful to contemplate biological triage—in effect, giving up on the species that are in the worst shape. Triage could turn today's biologists into modern-day Noahs, inviting selected species into the ark of preservation just as the biblical Noah loaded up his ark with the species that were saved from God's great flood. The University of Michigan's Michael Soulé, who is president of the Society for Conservation Biology, opposes the idea. He urges immediate action to save the most drastically endangered species, and he says, "I am not ready to have experts say thumbs up or thumbs down on some species without letting the public know." The Smithsonian's Thomas Lovejoy agrees. "This is biology's moment in history," he says. "We have to set our sights high and not be afraid of the cost, rather than to start admitting defeat and say triage is necessary." But most scientists share the view of Peter Raven of the Missouri Botanical Garden, who points out that species are perishing every day and that some species are going to die no matter what action the world's scientists and governments take. "What species survive is up to us, and we have to make hard choices," he says. "I call for intelligent decisions on which species to save and how to do it."

One course of action that is recommended by almost everyone who studies the extinction crisis is the development of a worldwide data base and information-sharing system so that scientists and environmentalists everywhere can pool information and work more efficiently toward common goals. One of these goals will very likely be the establishment of a global network of small, closely monitored parks and reserves in crucial areas of high biodiversity. Some experts feel that it would be easier to protect thousands of small, specialized parks than a few hundred large, all-purpose ones. In many countries, the trend in setting aside land for conservation purposes is toward little parks with complex or unique ecosystems and many species. A number of biologists are doing research to discover whether small reserves can be maintained in certain environments—for example, South American rainforests—while still preserving biodiversity.

Whatever course is followed by nations, conservation groups, and individuals who are concerned with the survival of this planet's rich variety of life-forms, one truth is inescapable: There is not much time. As Thomas Lovejoy says, "The problem is very big and the fuse is very short." And he adds, "I am utterly convinced that most of the great environmental struggles will be won or lost in the 1990s." The closing years of the 20th century and the start of the 21st will see either a new era of worldwide concern and cooperation that will halt the extermination of species or a descending spiral of destruction, death, and extinction.

HOW EVERYONE CAN HELP NOW

The following steps toward species preservation have been suggested by the World Wildlife Fund and other conservation and environmental groups.

- Do not buy wildlife products such as ivory, tortoiseshell, or wild furs. If you are interested in a product made from an animal or plant, be sure to ask what species it is made of and what its country of origin is. Be an informed consumer. Let merchants and manufacturers know that you care about wildlife protection.
- If you want a pet, adopt a cat or dog from an animal shelter. If you want a bird, lizard, or other exotic pet, insist on a captive-bred animal. Make certain that you know what species it is and where it was raised; check the endangered species list in your library or call the U.S. Fish and Wildlife Service if you have doubts.

This 2.5-acre (10-hectare) plot of Brazilian rainforest is part of the World Wildlife Fund's Minimum Critical Size project, which seeks to determine just how small an area of forest can still support various species.

- Get involved in wildlife study on a small scale. Birdwatching is a good place to start. Even city dwellers can soon learn to identify a surprisingly large number of bird species. Getting to know birds and their habits is one of the best ways to get interested in nature and conservation.
- Study the publications and programs of conservation groups and zoological societies and pick one or more to join. Support their work through donations, if you can afford them, or through volunteer work or purchases of goods such as T-shirts or pins that earn money for conservation projects.
- Write to your state's congresspersons and senators, urging them to support legislation that will protect fragile habitats and vulnerable species. Organize a petition drive for signatures to add to your letters, or make species preservation the subject of a school report or project.

APPENDIX: FOR MORE INFORMATION

U.S. and International Conservation Organizations

Center for Marine Conservation
1235 DeSales Street NW
Washington, DC 20036
(202) 429-5609

Cousteau Society
930 West 21st Street
Norfolk, VA 23517
(804) 627-1144

Earth Island Institute
300 Broadway, Suite 28
San Francisco, CA 94133
(415) 788-7324

Environmental Defense Fund
257 Park Avenue South
New York, NY 10010
(212) 505-2100

Friends of the Earth
218 D Street SE
Washington, DC 20003
(202) 544-2600

Greenpeace
1436 U Street NW
Washington, DC 20009
(202) 462-1177

Missouri Botanical Garden
P.O. Box 299
St. Louis, MO 63166-0299
(314) 577-5100

National Audubon Society
833 3rd Avenue
New York, NY 10022
(212) 832-3200

National Wildlife Federation
1412 16th Street NW
Washington, DC 20036
(202) 737-2024

Nature Conservancy International
1800 N. Kent Street, Suite 800
Arlington, VA 22209
(800) 628-6860

Rainforest Action Network
301 Broadway, Suite A
San Francisco, CA 94133
(415) 398-4404

Rainforest Alliance
270 Lafayette Street
New York, NY 10012
(212) 941-1900

Sierra Club
530 Bush Street
San Francisco, CA 94108
(415) 981-8634

United Nations Environment Program
1889 F Street NW
Washington, DC 20006
(202) 289-8456

Wilderness Society
1400 I Street NW
Washington, DC 20005
(202) 842-3200

World Society for the Protection of Animals
P.O. Box 190
29 Perkins Street
Boston, MA 02130
(617) 522-7000

World Wildlife Fund
1250 24th Street NW
Washington, DC 20037
(202) 293-4800

U.S. Government Agencies

Environmental Protection Agency
401 M Street SW
Washington, DC 20460
(202) 382-2090

National Forest Service
P.O. Box 2417
Washington, DC 20013
(202) 447-3760

National Park Service
P.O. Box 37127
Interior Building
Washington, DC 20013-7127
(202) 343-6843

U.S. Fish and Wildlife Service
Department of the Interior
1849 C Street NW
Washington, DC 20240
(202) 208-5634

FURTHER READING

Allaby, Michael, and James Lovelock. *The Great Extinction: The Solution to One of the Great Mysteries of Science—The Disappearance of the Dinosaurs.* Garden City, NY: Doubleday, 1983.

Amory, Cleveland. *Man Kind? Our Incredible War on Wildlife.* New York: HarperCollins, 1974.

Bergman, Charles. *Wild Echoes: Encounters with the Most Endangered Animals.* New York: McGraw-Hill, 1990.

Burton, John A. *Close to Extinction.* New York: Gloucester Press, 1988.

Burton, Maurice. *The World's Disappearing Wildlife.* London and New York: Marshall Cavendish, 1978.

Cadieux, Charles. *These Are the Endangered.* Washington, DC: Stone Wall Press, 1981.

Caras, Roger A. *Death as a Way of Life.* Boston: Little, Brown, 1970.

Carson, Rachel. *Silent Spring.* Boston: Houghton Mifflin, 1978.

Day, David. *The Doomsday Book of Animals: A Natural History of Vanished Species.* New York: Viking Penguin, 1981.

DiSilvestro, Roger L. *The Endangered Kingdom: The Struggle to Save America's Wildlife.* New York: Wiley, 1989.

Durrell, Lee. *State of the Ark: An Atlas of Conservation in Action.* Garden City, NY: Doubleday, 1986.

Ehrlich, Paul, and Anne Ehrlich. *Extinction: Causes and Consequences of the Disappearance of Species.* New York: Random House, 1981.

Eldredge, Niles. *Life Pulse: Episodes from the Story of the Fossil Record.* New York: Facts on File, 1987.

———. *Time Frames.* New York: Simon & Schuster, 1984.

Fitzgerald, Sarah. *International Wildlife Trade: Whose Business Is It?* Washington, DC: World Wildlife Fund, 1989.

Gore, Rick. "Extinctions." *National Geographic* (June 1989): 662–99.

Gould, Stephen Jay. "Continuity." In *The Flamingo's Smile.* New York: Norton, 1985.

———. "The Great Dying." In *Ever Since Darwin.* New York: Norton, 1977.

———. "Sex, Drugs, Disasters, and the Extinction of Dinosaurs." In *The Flamingo's Smile.* New York: Norton, 1985.

Hoage, R. J., ed. *Animal Extinctions: What Everyone Should Know.* Washington, DC: Smithsonian Institution Press, 1985.

Johanson, Donald, and Maitland Edey. *Lucy: The Beginnings of Humankind.* New York: Simon & Schuster, 1981.

Lampton, Christopher. *Endangered Species.* New York: Watts, 1988.

Leakey, Richard, and Roger Lewin. *Mass Extinction: One Theory of Why the Dinosaurs Vanished.* New York: Watts, 1986.

———. *The People of the Lake: Mankind and Its Beginnings.* Garden City, NY: Doubleday, 1978.

Kaufman, Les and Kenneth Mallory. *The Last Extinction.* Cambridge: MIT Press, 1986.

Lewis, Thomas A. "How Did the Giants Die?" *International Wildlife* (September–October 1987): 4–12.

McClung, Robert M. *Vanishing Wildlife of Latin America.* New York: Morrow, 1981.

McKibben, Bill. *The End of Nature.* New York: Random House, 1989.

May, Robert M. "How Many Species Are There on Earth?" *Science* (September 16, 1988): 1441–49.

Mohlenbrock, Robert H. *Where Have All the Wildflowers Gone?* New York: Macmillan, 1983.

Mowat, Farley. *Sea of Slaughter.* New York: Bantam Books, 1986.

Muller, Richard. *Nemesis.* New York: Weidenfeld & Nicolson, 1988.

Myers, Norman, ed. *Gaia: An Atlas of Planet Management.* New York: Doubleday, 1984.

Nichol, John. *The Animal Smugglers and Other Wildlife Traders.* New York: Facts on File, 1987.

Nilsson, Greta. *The Endangered Species Handbook.* Washington, DC: Animal Welfare Institute, 1983.

Robert, Leslie. "Hard Choices Ahead on Biodiversity." *Science* (September 30, 1988): 1759–1961.

Stanley, Steven M. *Extinction.* New York: Scientific American Library and Freeman, 1987.

Stewart, Darryl. *From the Edge of Extinction: The Fight to Save Endangered Species.* New York and London: Methuen, 1978.

Stonehouse, Bernard. *Saving the Animals: The World Wildlife Fund Book of Conservation.* New York: Macmillan, 1981.

Tongren, Sally. *To Keep Them Alive: Wild Animal Breeding.* New York: Dembner Books, 1985.

U.S. Fish and Wildlife Service. *Endangered Species Listing Handbook.* Washington, DC: USFWS, 1989.

Whitfield, Philip. *Can the Whales Be Saved? Questions About the Natural World and Threats to Its Survival Answered by the Natural History Museum.* New York: Viking Kestrel, 1989.

Wilson, Edward O. "Threats to Biodiversity." *Scientific American* (September 1989): 108–16.

World Wildlife Fund. *Guide to Endangered Species of North America.* Washington, DC: Beacham, 1989.

Periodicals

Audubon Activist Newsletter. Published 6 times a year by the National Audubon Society, New York, NY.

Earth Island Journal. Published 4 times a year by the Earth Island Institute, San Francisco, CA.

Greenpeace. Published 6 times a year by Greenpeace, Washington, DC.

National Wildlife. Published 6 times a year by the National Wildlife Federation, Washington, DC.

Sierra. Published 6 times a year by the Sierra Club, San Francisco, CA.

Traffic (USA): A Newsletter on International Trade in Wildlife and Wildlife Products. Published 4 times a year by World Wildlife Fund, Washington, DC.

World Rainforest Report. Published 4 times a year by the Rainforest Action Network, San Francisco, CA.

GLOSSARY

biodiversity The genetic variety in living **species**; the more different species there are, the greater the degree of biodiversity.

biosphere That part of the earth and its atmosphere inhabited by living organisms.

ecology The study of the interrelationships of species in an **ecosystem**.

ecosystem An area in which species interact with and are interdependent upon each other and the environment. The actual size of a given ecosystem depends on perspective; in discussions about species, such as humans, that range over the whole globe, the earth can be considered a single ecosystem, but in discussions about mites or beetles, a single tree in a tropical rainforest may be a self-contained ecosystem.

ecotourism Ecological tourism; the use of wildlife and wild **habitats** to attract tourists or visitors (and the money they spend).

endemic Restricted to a single, limited range; found nowhere else.

evolution The idea, first expressed by the naturalist Charles Darwin, that all life-forms, both living and extinct, are related to one another and descended from the same ancestral forms. An important aspect of the theory of evolution is that species change over time because of minor variations in individual organisms. See **natural selection**.

extinction The death and disappearance, for all time, of all living members of a species or larger group of creatures. A species is considered extinct for all practical purposes when some representatives remain alive but are unable to breed—for example, if all are male.

fauna Animal species.

flora Plant species.

fossil Remains or imprints of ancient life preserved in the earth, including bones and other body parts, eggs, and other traces. The term is usually applied to remains that are at least 6,000 years old; most fossils are considerably older.

geology The study of the earth's formation, development, and composition.

habitat The kind of environment in which an organism lives, such as a rainforest, shallow freshwater pool, or desert.

mass extinction The dying-off of many species or families of species at about the same time. The fossil record reveals that life on earth has undergone at least 12 mass extinctions, 5 of which were so severe that they greatly reduced **biodiversity**.

megafauna Literally, "big animals." Used to refer to animals whose body weight generally exceeds 100 pounds (37.3 kilograms).

natural selection The process, first suggested by Charles Darwin, by which variations in individual organisms create new species. The principle of natural selection states that variations that improve an organism's chances of survival will be transmitted to future generations because that organism will be more likely to live long and reproduce. Variations that work against an organism's chances of survival will not be as readily transmitted because that organism will not be as likely to reproduce.

paleontology The study of past life-forms by means of **fossils**.

poaching Illegal hunting.

punctuated equilibrium A theory developed by scientists Niles Eldredge and Stephen Jay Gould maintaining that the number of species remains relatively unchanged over long periods of time and then increases rapidly in short bursts of **speciation**, often following a phase of extinctions.

range Where a species lives in geographic terms; its distribution on the planet.

speciation The process of new species formation.

species All organisms that, under natural conditions, can breed and produce offspring that are in turn capable of reproducing. Members of a species are more genetically similar to each other than to members of other species.

sustainable use Sustainable development; managing wildlife resources in such a way that they provide income without being destroyed or depleted.

taxonomy The system created by scientists for organizing and naming plants and animals. Categories used by taxonomists range from kingdoms—the largest category—through phyla, classes, orders, families, genera, and species.

INDEX

PICTURE CREDITS

Rob Bierregaard/World Wildlife Fund: pp. 66, 67 (top), 71, 107, 110; © Rob Bierregaard/World Wildlife Fund: p. 67 (bottom); © Y. Blanco-Castillo/ Greenpeace: p. 83; David Clendenen/U.S. Fish and Wildlife Service: p. 70 (bottom); © Dennis Dagnan/Greenpeace: p. 100; Luther C. Goldman/U.S. Fish and Wildlife Service: pp. 14, 74; Greenpeace: pp. 50, 59, 76, 86, 88, 91, 102; © Greenpeace: p. 68; Greenpeace/Delforre: p. 12; © Greenpeace/ Grace: p. 70 (top); Greenpeace/Morgan: cover; © Greenpeace/Parker: p. 78; Henry Doorly Zoo, Omaha: pp. 69 (top and bottom), 105; © William Laros/ Greenpeace: p. 65; Library of Congress: pp. 26, 31, 33, 36; Royal Tyrrell Museum/Alberta Culture and Multiculturalism: pp. 38, 43, 47, 72; Linda L. Sims: p. 23; Smithsonian Institution: pp. 16 (neg. # 619C), 53 (neg. # 77-8474), 56 (neg. # 77-78-8A); U.S. Department of the Interior/Bureau of Land Management: pp. 95, 97; U.S. Fish and Wildlife Service: pp. 19, 62

Illustration by Gary Tong: p. 32

ABOUT THE AUTHOR

REBECCA STEFOFF is a Philadelphia-based freelance writer and editor who has published more than 40 nonfiction books for young adults. Many of her books deal with geography and exploration, and she takes an active interest in environmental issues and global ecology. She has also served as the editorial director of Chelsea House's *Places and Peoples of the World* and *Let's Discover Canada* series. Stefoff received her M.A. and Ph.D. degrees in English from the University of Pennsylvania, where she taught for three years.

ABOUT THE EDITOR

RUSSELL E. TRAIN, currently chairman of the board of directors of the World Wildlife Fund and The Conservation Foundation, has had a long and distinguished career of government service under three presidents. In 1957 President Eisenhower appointed him a judge of the United States Tax Court. He served Lyndon Johnson on the National Water Commission. Under Richard Nixon he became under secretary of the Interior and, in 1970, first chairman of the Council on Environmental Quality. From 1973 to 1977 he served as administrator of the Environmental Protection Agency. Train is also a trustee or director of the African Wildlife Foundation; the Alliance to Save Energy; the American Conservation Association; Citizens for Ocean Law; Clean Sites, Inc.; the Elizabeth Haub Foundation; the King Mahendra Trust for Nature Conservation (Nepal); Resources for the Future; the Rockefeller Brothers Fund; the Scientists' Institute for Public Information; the World Resources Institute; and Union Carbide and Applied Energy Services, Inc. Train is a graduate of Princeton and Columbia Universities, a veteran of World War II, and currently resides in the District of Columbia.